Frank, Sammy, Marlon & Me

Adventures in Paradise with the Celebrity Set

Frank, Sammy, Marlon & Me

Adventures in Paradise with the Celebrity Set

Eddie Sherman

WATERMARK
PUBLISHING

© 2006 Eddie Sherman

All rights reserved. No part of this book may be reproduced in any form or by any electronic or mechanical means, including information retrieval systems, without prior written permission from the publisher, except for brief passages quoted in reviews.

ISBN 0-9779143-8-0

Library of Congress Control Number: 2006935586

All author royalties earned from book sales are donated to the Rehabilitation Hospital of the Pacific.

Design
Leo Gonzalez

Production
Wendy Wakabayashi

Photo credits as indicated or from the Eddie Sherman Collection

Watermark Publishing
1088 Bishop Street, Suite 310
Honolulu, HI 96813
Telephone: Toll-free 1-866-900-BOOK
Web site: www.bookshawaii.net
email: sales@bookshawaii.net

Printed in Korea

Contents

Foreword		1
Introduction		3
1	Eddie: The Orphanage	6
2	Eddie: Hawaii	15
3	Arthur Godfrey	34
4	Albert Finney	39
5	Bette Midler	43
6	Bob Hope	50
7	Don Ho	53
8	Donald O'Connor & Rocky Marciano	56
9	Elvis Presley & Colonel Tom Parker	76
10	Frank Sinatra	82
11	Henry J. Kaiser	91
12	Jack Lord	97
13	Jack Paar	107
14	Jack Soo	111
15	James Clavell	114
16	John Ford	118
17	Judy Garland	124
18	Kui Lee & Hal Wallis	128
19	Larry Mehau	134
20	Lenny Bruce	142
21	Marlon Brando	146
22	Marty Rackin	177
23	Max Winter	179
24	Mike Todd & Joe Resnick	185
25	Muhammad Ali & Angelo Dundee	188
26	Otto Preminger & Burgess Meredith	192
27	Peggy Ryan	196
28	Red Skelton	199
29	Richard Boone	204
30	Sammy Amalu	207
31	Sammy Davis, Jr.	211
32	Sophia Loren	215
33	Sugar Ray Robinson	217
34	Tommy Sands	220
35	Walter Dornberger	224
36	Walter Winchell	227
37	Short Takes	232
Epilogue		237
Index		242

For Patty, my inspiration and the love of my life

Foreword

When Eddie asked me to write the foreword for this book, I asked him, "What's a foreword?"

He smiled. "It's the opposite of backward!"

You would have to know Eddie to understand his sharp wit and keen sense of humor. Life with Eddie has always been entertaining. He is endlessly curious and sees things with a fresh outlook. And he always has a story to tell.

As a young man, Eddie was a stand-up comedian, and I believe this training is the basis for his witty retorts.

Many of you may not know the real Eddie Sherman. He was born Eli Sherman, the only child of an immigrant couple from Russia. When his parents split up, six-year-old Eli was placed in an orphanage. Eli grew up alone and insecure. His mother would visit him at the home, but he rarely saw his father and has just a vague memory of him.

Fighting became a big part of Eli's childhood. It was, as he says today, all about survival. He sought to win the favor of his contemporaries by being the tough guy—using his fists to gain admiration and respect from others.

As a young lad, Eli sold newspapers in Harvard Square. He saved his money and would hop on the backs of trucks or street cars to hitch rides to the vaudeville shows playing in Boston. For less than a dollar, he could see a show and buy a hotdog. This was his escape from his lonely world.

One of Eli's favorite performers was Eddie Cantor, the legendary star of stage, radio and movies. Seeing Cantor's magnetic performances was what sparked Eli's love of entertainment. He realized that he could get the love and attention he sorely missed through performing for others. Applause, he figured, meant acceptance. Suddenly, it all came together for this young boy who sat entranced in the darkened theater.

Eli Sherman would change his name to Eddie Sherman in honor of his beloved Eddie Cantor.

Years later, at the Lau Yee Chai Restaurant and Nightclub in Honolulu, Eddie Sherman the stand-up comedian would perform a blackface record pantomime act, mimicking the Eddie Cantor routine he saw as a lad in Boston.

I became aware of Eddie Sherman while growing up in Hawaii and reading his columns in the *Honolulu Advertiser*. His columns brought the glamour of show business and celebrities right into our homes. His writing made us feel like we had actually come face to face with these famous stars and luminaries.

They say there are no coincidences. My meeting with Eddie in September of 1996, instead, was destiny calling. My $5 bid to dance with him at a celebrity auction changed both of our lives. We were married in the spring of 1997.

Eddie is a great storyteller. During our dates, he would relate these delightful stories of people he had met and interviewed throughout his career.

Whenever Eddie told his stories at dinner parties or in informal conversations with friends, there was always the same comment: "Why don't you put this into a book?" It was a subject that we discussed quite often, and finally we decided it was time to share his stories with the world.

This book has been a labor of love for Eddie. Reliving each of the stories by putting them on paper has been a satisfying and fun experience for him.

I know that you will enjoy the stories you are about to read. They are a compilation of a lifetime of work, and the celebrity friendships he made here in Hawaii.

Aloha,
Patty Sherman

INTRODUCTION

"Hey, Sailor..."

Do you remember the first time you met an honest-to-goodness, larger-than-life celebrity? Some people may have a story like that to tell. Maybe it involved bumping into an inebriated Hollywood star at a Los Angeles nightclub or getting a basketball legend's autograph at a book signing.

I'll have to wager, though, that my first encounter with a celebrity was more intimate than most. After all, it's not every day that you get to hold the derrière of a ravishing major Hollywood actress.

I guess I'd better explain.

The year was 1942 and I had just been given an honorable medical discharge from the U.S Coast Guard. I dislocated my left shoulder during basic training in Algiers, Louisiana. The Coast Guard refused to operate because I had a history of previous shoulder dislocations and, in fact, I had surgery on my shoulder before entering the service. I argued that since they examined and accepted me, why shouldn't they be responsible for fixing my shoulder? But my efforts fell on deaf ears.

Here I was, just seventeen years old, and my dream of serving in the military was already dashed to pieces. I hopped on a bus back to Boston, my hometown, with no job prospects and only a few dollars in my pocket. At least I had permission to wear the Coast Guard uniform for a couple months.

On my way home, I decided to stop in New York for a day or two. I had never been there in my life. All alone in the Big Apple! I felt like just a tiny grain of sand on the huge beach of mammoth Manhattan.

Most people in New York have this in common: they walk. A lot. Everybody does it, and so did I. It was exhilarating! The sights, sounds, smells and feel of New York—everything was just throbbing with excitement.

While I was strolling along in the Times Square area, a car suddenly pulled up to the curb. A man leaned out the window and yelled, "Hey, sailor. Would you come over here for a minute?"

So I did. "What's up?" I asked.

The gentleman told me he was a publicity man for a motion picture company. A major film star was arriving at Grand Central Station, he said, and he was trying to round up as many military folks as possible for a photo session with her. He gave me a few dollars for a taxi and told me exactly what track the train was coming in on. Then the car sped off.

I had nothing better to do, so off I went to meet a movie star. The greeting party was easy to find—it was quite a crowd—and all branches of the services were represented. There were about thirty of us in all.

And suddenly there she was: Merle Oberon, stepping off the train—beautifully dressed, oozing glamour and sophistication.

She was one of the major screen stars of that era. I had seen some of her films and was a big fan. I especially enjoyed her in *Wuthering Heights*. She was so sultry and exotic looking. I had never before seen a famous film star in person. This was exciting!

Before Oberon got off the train, the man who asked me to come to the station came over and selected a soldier and myself to be the ones to make a "seat" for Oberon. I'd like to think it was my chiseled good looks that landed me this opportunity, but more likely it was because I was one of the smaller guys in the group.

The soldier and I locked wrists. As Miss Oberon was brought to us, we lowered our hands and she sat on our little "seat." She put her arms on our shoulders and smiled broadly as we lifted her up.

She smelled like flowers. So delicate and dainty! Camera flashbulbs went off like fireflies.

"It's a real pleasure to be holding you, Miss Oberon," I said. "I have enjoyed your movies."

"Thank you," she replied, smiling sweetly.

And then, just like that, it was over. Oberon was quickly escorted out of the station to a waiting limo.

    I never got to meet Merle Oberon again. As fate would have it, however, this chance encounter was just a preview of things to come. Never in my wildest dreams did I think I'd someday cross paths with the likes of Elvis Presley, Frank Sinatra, Judy Garland and Rocky Marciano. I never imagined that I would someday go sailing with Albert Finney, and become buddies with guys like Sammy Davis, Jr., and Marlon Brando.

    But it all happened. These stories, and many more, are all here in this book.

    Enjoy!

    Eddie Sherman

ONE

Eddie: The Orphanage

She thought she was doing the right thing. I understand that now. Back then, at the time, it was all about survival, about finding ways to stay alive. Still, all I can remember is the sadness of being abandoned. You see, I was placed in an orphanage in 1929, when I was six years old.

With a heavy heart, my poor mother, Bessie, left her little boy in a place she thought would be safe: an institution for youngsters. At least I would have a warm place to sleep and have food to eat.

Of course, my thoughts then were not of warm beds and hot meals, but of being wrenched away from my mother. The memories still haunt me today.

I was angry at the world for suddenly putting me in a strange place where I didn't know a soul. I was alone, bewildered—an outcast living in a prison without bars. I felt so unwanted, unloved.

Plain and simple, I felt discarded.

Every night, the tears burned my eyes. How my heart ached for my mother! I would look forward to each Saturday, when she would come to visit me. Although we could barely communicate, she was there. She was my mother and I did love her so very much.

My recollections of my "home" of that time are not very pleasant. The worst times were at night. Many of the boys would cry in their cots, their faces buried in their pillows. I clutched my blankets and dreamed of my mother and the few moments we would spend together. Where was she? Was she all right? How much time before I would see her again? After all, she was all I had.

As the years passed, I learned more about my parents. They were

Russian immigrants of the Jewish faith who came to America in the early 1900s to escape the cold brutality and persecution of the Russian Cossacks. They spoke no English and had little education. They couldn't read or write. They fled Russia, along with thousands of other people, when the Cossacks devastated their farms and villages.

My parents settled in the slum areas of Boston. The only work opportunities available to them were in dilapidated sweatshops, where they toiled twelve to fifteen hours every day. No air conditioning in the summer, no heat in the winter. My parents were barely surviving, but they were safe from the Cossacks.

They were in America, land of the free.

My mother once told me a story about how she walked miles in blizzards in Boston, just to save the nickel it would have cost to ride a streetcar. That's just the way it was back then. Money was so important, so elusive. To spend a penny was almost sacrilegious.

My father? He was a ne'er-do-well. He worked hard to earn his wages, but he was seldom home. He would be away, in fact, for days and weeks at a time. My memory of him is minimal.

In time, my mother had to figure out how she was going to raise her little boy alone. She finally divorced my father. Back then, this was a very courageous thing to do, but my mother had guts. She was a single parent long before it became acceptable. She felt it was better to go on alone, although thankfully she did receive some help from relatives.

Placing me in an orphanage was a decision that I know she anguished over. What mother wouldn't? Life, it is said, sometimes pushes us to the limits of our own endurance. So Bessie made her choice, and the course of my early life was set.

Ironically, it was in this orphanage that I discovered one of my early goals in life.

The home had a huge barracks that served as both a recreation center and gathering place for all the kids. A small, black, pot-bellied stove was our only source of heat during the winter months. We all gathered around it to keep ourselves from freezing.

One night not long after I'd moved in, one of the older kids put a pair of boxing gloves on me at the recreation center. Now, I was a puny guy, and the gloves weighed my hands down. I could barely hold them up! All I could hear were the sounds of cheering and yelling. Everyone was egging me on, shouting, "Fight!"

I had no idea what was going on. The only thing I did know, in fact, was that I was suddenly the center of attention—and I loved it! Then someone shoved me into the ring. I saw another boy with gloves on coming straight at me, so I took a big swing. I was excited and anxious; and I put all I had into this one punch. I knew I would connect and send him flying across the ring, and I would be the hero of the night. I had to do it!

The momentum of my swing carried the full weight of my body and propelled me forward. The problem was, I missed my target and wound up plunging across the room. I crashed into that black stove in the corner. My head hit the hot metal, and I went sprawling onto the floor.

No! This couldn't be happening! My one chance! I saw my dreams dashed as the room filled with laughter.

Quickly, I got back on my feet. My head was throbbing, and I was still dizzy and disoriented, but someone guided me and pointed me toward my opponent (who, it turned out, was as scared as I was). I figured I had nothing to lose, so I mustered all the strength I had left and charged after him with another huge swing. This time, I connected. The poor guy went down and stayed there for a minute or so.

The acclaim I felt at that moment was like a drug. Suddenly, I couldn't get enough of all the attention and affection from the kids. With one wild swing, my life had taken a turn. I was suddenly recognized and accepted. I was now a "fighter," and this, I believed, would be my ticket out of this sad life.

After that initial baptism of minor glory, I had many, many fights. In school. After school. With anybody. I loved it. I was like an animal looking for trouble. I reveled in the action. I even fought in smokers, where the winners got prizes. I took anything they had to offer.

I lived this way until I was about thirteen. In hindsight, I can see the fighting was a release for my hostilities and anger. It was my way of righting the wrongs that were being done to me, or so I thought. Talk about being misguided! Of course, back then, there were no role models for me to emulate. It was survival of the fittest, and during those formative years, survival was the name of the game.

When I was thirteen, the orphanage closed and all the kids were farmed out to foster homes. The only home I knew was now being taken out of my life. Once again, another adjustment had to be made. I simply blocked out any emotions that I might have had.

Being at the mercy of others is a terrible thing when you are so young. There is very little self-esteem that you can have when you are constantly being reminded you exist solely because of the generosity of others.

I remember quite well one of the foster homes I was put into. There were three children in the family. The welfare system was paying them to take me in, so I was income to them. I was also a burden, another mouth to feed, and they let me know it. I was not really wanted there. The only thing that mattered was the monthly check that came with me.

The Green family was considered between lower and middle class. Back then, that meant looking for the next bit of food to eat and a way to heat your home during Boston's cold, freezing winters. This was during the Great Depression. No extras. People were selling apples on street corners for five cents, and you were lucky to have three squares. The Greens were always looking for ways to make an extra buck, and taking in foster children was a financial advantage. There were many families that did this back then to make ends meet. I suppose it still happens today.

I was treated as an outsider, and the family had great disdain for me. The children looked down on me as that strange kid who their parents took in. The adults, meanwhile, would tolerate my presence—but there was never any caring. They hardly talked to me or gave me the time of day. They resented me taking up an extra bed and eating their food.

Mornings were the worst. Mrs. Green would yell at us to get up, and the frantic day would begin. I needed to go to the bathroom, but the pecking order had been established—the three Green children always went first—and so I had to wait my turn. The children knew of my needs, of course, and would deliberately take their time getting washed up. By the time the bathroom was available for me, Mrs. Green was shouting last call for breakfast. I had to make a choice, and I always chose to eat.

Breakfast was gobbled down in seconds. Yes, my bladder was ready to burst, but my hunger was tremendous! I was a growing boy and always hungry—it seemed there was never enough food! Today my wife sometimes wonders why I eat so quickly. She says no one is going to take the food away from me. Part of this is probably a throwback to my childhood, when it was everyone for himself. Survival, remember, survival. I felt that no one was going to take care of me, so I had to do it myself.

With the last mouthful of food still in my mouth, I would run out the back door to pee in the bushes on my way to school. Eventually, this routine weakened my kidneys and I began wetting my bed. At this age, to be peeing in bed was horrific. I tried to hide it, but the mother of the house would obviously discover this sin and was furious with me. I thought she was a witch!

When she found out the bed had been urinated on, she would beat me. Sometimes it was with a dog strap; sometimes it was an iron stove poker. This was a very dark time for me. I was stuck with this cruel family, with nowhere to turn and no way to fight back.

Enter my angel of mercy.

In my child's eyes, she was the most beautiful person in the whole wide world! Her name was Marjorie Ellis, and I will never forget her. She is gone now, as are the witches and predators of my early childhood. But Marjorie will live on in my heart and mind. And I will continue to tell her story to encourage and give hope to others.

Was she that special? I thought so. I had never had such kindness shown to me! Her kindness, in fact, was almost foreign to me. I had grown so accustomed to the callousness of the world around me.

Marjorie, then in her forties, was my sixth-grade teacher.

I attended the Roger Wolcott School, an old red brick building in Dorchester, a suburb of Boston. I remember Marjorie reading books to the class, and the stories would transport us out of our dismal lives to places we could only dream of. One story in particular made quite an impression on me. The book was titled *Kimo*, and it was about a little boy who lived in Hawaii. What a strange, yet beautiful, land this book told about!

I loved being in Marjorie's class. She was so kind and understanding, and always captivated us with her beautiful smile. The need I had to be loved and cared for as a child was met by this soft-spoken, kind, caring woman. (Notice how some memories fade away to some unknown place in time, while others are burned in like a mental branding, so we never forget. My memories of Marjorie are as fresh in my mind today as they were when I was a child.)

One morning, Marjorie was walking up and down the aisles of the classroom, checking each student's work. Everyone was busy trying to complete the assignment. She stopped at my desk to look over my shoulder. I winced when she placed her hand on my back.

"What's wrong?" she asked.

"Nothing," I replied. She touched my back again, and I flinched in pain once more.

She pulled up my shirt and saw the crusted blood over my back—the result of the morning's beating with the iron poker and dog strap.

Marjorie personally marched me right down to the principal's office to show him my wounds. The very next day, I was out of the Greens' house and placed in another foster home. There would be a total of four homes I would live in during my youth. I was a transient who moved from place to place. Nothing was ever stable. I lived with strangers who took me in only because the welfare paid them. Parental love was nonexistent.

Still, I was eternally grateful to Marjorie. In my childlike way, I promised her the moon for saving me.

Later on in life, as a successful columnist in Hawaii, I arranged for Marjorie to visit me in the Islands. I wanted her to see the land of *Kimo* that she introduced me to in her class. I purchased her plane tickets and got her two weeks at the Kahala Hilton—on the house.

When she arrived in Honolulu, I greeted her with leis galore. She looked like a dignitary arriving at the airport! I wined and dined her. She was taken to every top-notch place in town. I couldn't do enough for her. We had lunch with an admiral from Pearl Harbor and the Commanding General of Hickam Air Force Base. The Mayor of Honolulu gave her a proclamation. She met John Burns, then governor of Hawaii. Marjorie was even made an honorary chiefess at the Polynesian Cultural Center.

Yes, Marjorie was seeing it all with the kid from Dorchester whom she had saved. She was interviewed by the media, and our friendship was well documented.

On one of our tours around the island, I asked Marjorie if she had a favorite actor. Her reply was Richard Boone. "Oh, I just love his acting," she said.

Wouldn't you know it, Boone was living in Hawaii at the time. He and I, in fact, were good friends. We even wrote some scripts together that didn't pan out.

Richard came to Hawaii because he wanted his son Peter to attend Punahou, which is one of Hawaii's most prestigious schools. I told him about Marjorie and asked if he would be her surprise "date" when we went to the Kahala Hilton for dinner and a show. Richard readily and happily agreed.

Over a leisurely meal that evening, Marjorie and I talked about her day's adventures. Suddenly, a very large man materialized behind her, and a distinguished, low voice asked, "Are you Marjorie Ellis?" She turned and looked at Richard's rugged, famous face.

"I'm your dinner companion for the evening," he said, smiling.

Marjorie was absolutely shocked. Her mouth dropped, and her eyes bulged with almost a look of horror. I thought she was going to faint.

She could not believe this was actually happening.

No question, this was one of the most thrilling moments in

Marjorie's life. It certainly was one of mine, as I beamed with joy, seeing her happiness. And Richard, bless his heart, played his role to the hilt. He was a very charming companion for Marjorie.

What Marjorie did for me those days of my youth could never be repaid. She taught me more than lessons from a school textbook. She taught me life lessons that would stay with me forever.

She was my savior.

During this period, I continued to fight at every opportunity. Again, it was probably my suppressed hostility being released. I "trained" at the Y. I exercised constantly. I hung out in boxing gyms, watching the pros work out and asking questions. I sparred every chance I got and boxed in smokers around the city.

I became friendly with a boxing trainer at the Y. His name was Ruby Hootstein. Thinking I had some potential, Ruby began to give me instruction. He had trained a fighter by the name of Mike Kaplan, who was from my neighborhood. Mike was a pro, a local hero. Eventually, Mike landed a non-title fight with world lightweight champion Fritzie Zivik. Because of his success and his potential, Mike was lured away from Ruby and signed with other managers. This broke Ruby's heart because he practically raised the young man.

When Mike fought Zivik, Ruby invited me to be his guest at the Boston Garden to see the fight. Kaplan beat the champion in a ten-round decision. Ruby was happy for Mike, but was saddened by being deserted by him.

"If you keep training me, one day I'll be able to beat Kaplan," I remember telling Ruby. But Ruby decided not to try again—with anybody. He was just too brokenhearted.

One afternoon when I was sixteen, I was in a pickup baseball game. I attempted to steal a base, sliding into it head first. While diving at the bag, I somehow landed on my left shoulder. It dislocated.

The pain was excruciating! I was taken to a hospital. After that, the dislocations became frequent. They even occurred during boxing matches. Eventually, I was forced to have the shoulder operated on.

Not knowing any better, I returned to the gym without giving my shoulder time to heal properly. The result was another operation. And that was the end of my boxing dreams.

TWO

Eddie: Hawaii

The year was 1941, and World War II was raging in Europe. I was a teenaged kid from Boston who wanted to escape from my confined world. So I enlisted in the Coast Guard. What a glorious time, I thought—traveling by train down the East Coast to boot camp in Algiers, Louisiana, just across the river from New Orleans. What an adventure! There were sights I had never witnessed before, and the accommodations were certainly better than my previous living conditions. It was just an exciting opportunity to see some of the country, and from such a wonderful vantage point.

After only a few months in Coast Guard boot camp, however, I dislocated my left shoulder again.

I'd thought the previous operation had fixed my shoulder, but sadly I was wrong. Worse, the Coast Guard gave me a medical discharge because I had already had surgery before enlisting, and they refused to operate. I pleaded with them, but to no avail.

It was another long train ride back to Boston. Instead of excitement and anticipation, however, this time I felt very discouraged. I had no job and didn't know what to do. I wound up hanging around the pool halls of my old neighborhood.

Many of my friends were finding employment in national defense jobs. So, I applied for a position as a sheet metal helper at the Boston Navy Yard and was surprised when I was accepted. But not to work in Boston.

I was asked to go to a place I had never heard of before— Pearl Harbor.

It was a job. And it was another opportunity to escape and stretch my horizons.

One Sunday afternoon, I was riding around with some fellas from the neighborhood in a broken-down jalopy. The radio announcer started shouting excitedly, "Pearl Harbor has been attacked!"

One of the guys looked at me and said, "Hey, Sherman, ain't that where you're going?"

I grunted. "Like hell I am," I replied.

After that, I tried to get out of my commitment. Some of my pals called me "chicken." Finally, I gave up. I knew I was bound for Pearl Harbor.

A few weeks later, I received my orders to leave Boston and take a train to San Francisco. Another adventure—chugging across the country all alone. I marveled at the vastness of America. I checked into a hotel and was told to await further orders. Two weeks later, in the dead of night, I got a call telling me to take a taxi to the waterfront and board a ship.

It turned out the ship was the former luxury liner *Lurline*, which had been converted into a troop transport vessel. It was the largest mass of metal I had ever seen. To me, it looked like the size of a New York skyscraper.

The sounds of the dock and the nighttime activities on the ship were exciting. In the vast hold of the ship, the roar of the masses sounded like a stadium crowd cheering a touchdown.

Bunk beds hung from the ceiling, one on top of the other. Men were packed in like sardines. They smoked, played card games, rolled dice, cursed, argued, fought and consumed the alcoholic beverages that had been smuggled aboard. These men were rough and tough with one thing in common: we were all leaving "America" for a strange land called Hawaii.

What if we're captured? *Great*, I thought. *Another adventure.* It would still be better than living in Boston.

At the same time, of course, there was an empty, lonely feeling of being away from families and familiar surroundings.

It was very difficult to get any sleep that first night on the ship.

There was a very thick sense of nervousness and edgy tension. I remember the sounds of the guys' nervous laughter, trying not to show their apprehension about what would happen next. This was immediately after the Pearl Harbor attack, remember, and everyone seemed revved up and eager for a fight. Still, there was also the gnawing fear what might lie ahead.

The following morning, I awoke with a huge appetite as well as a curiosity to find out what was going on. I was anxious to go atop and see what I could see.

When I got on deck, the salty sea breeze filled my lungs with fresh air. What I saw before me, however, took my breath away: all around us, as far as my eyes could see, the ocean was filled with ships of all sizes and shapes, to the left, to the right, in front of us and behind us—an incredible armada of American power, zigzagging to avoid possible enemy torpedoes.

On deck one morning, I looked up at the crow's nest—the small platform high above the deck. An older Navy officer wearing a black eye patch, with lots of scrambled eggs on his cap, seemed to be in command of a group of men.

They were taking turns looking through the lens of a motion picture camera. I was told the gentleman with the eye patch was Rear Admiral John Ford, the legendary film director. While in the Navy, he was filming the epic *The Battle of Midway*.

Years later, I interviewed him on his yacht, the *Araner*, which was then berthed at the Ala Wai Yacht Harbor in Honolulu. More on that later.

Eventually, we reached the Hawaiian island of Oahu. The *Lurline* glided into Honolulu Harbor on a bright, sunny day with the trade winds gently blowing.

It was one of the most beautiful sights I had ever seen in my life.

When we arrived, we saw a troupe of lovely Island maidens swaying to and fro, moving their hands gracefully like palm trees in the breeze. A band played music unlike anything I had heard before. I thought, "We must be very special to be welcomed like this."

This daydreaming didn't last long. We marched off the ship

into waiting cattle-type transportation that deposited us at Civilian Housing Number Three, or CHA-3, in the Damon Tract area. Just a few months earlier, this land had been a sugarcane field right outside Pearl Harbor. Suddenly, military housing had sprung up, and we were among the first tenants.

Even though I was a stranger in a strange land, not knowing a soul, I was surprisingly happy. I had a job, earning $1.25 an hour as a sheet metal helper. It was the most money I had ever made in my life. A small fortune!

We actually arrived at the beginning of Honolulu's rainy season. After the first downpour we experienced, CHA-3, which had no paved roads or sidewalks, was like one big mud hole!

For recreation, it was mostly drinking, gambling and fighting. I remember going to a dance at the old Civic Auditorium on King Street. Basically, I just stood around and watched. I saw a handsome officer in uniform, a Clark Gable look-alike, ask a local woman for a dance. She was fat, with uncombed hair and missing front teeth. Describing her as "ugly" would actually be a compliment.

She looked up at this officer and arrogantly sneered, "No, t'anks." Back then, on the Mainland, with men so scarce, the ladies would have eaten that officer alive.

My sometimes-refuge in those days was the Waikiki Theater. I went there at every opportunity. I had never seen such a beautiful movie establishment. Edwin Sawtelle played the huge organ in a short concert before movies started. Fake, lush tropical vegetation and trees decorated the theater. Twinkling lights in the ceiling dotted a darkened "sky," and clouds appeared to drift by. It was an enchanting experience. I felt as though it was my own private hideaway. (Sadly, the theater no longer exists. In its place are more tourist shops. Progress?)

Martial law reigned supreme during World War II. Everyone had to carry a gas mask, and all money had the word "Hawaii" stamped on the bills. In the event the Territory was invaded—and there were persistent rumors that it would happen—the money would become worthless.

I remember rumbling along on the bus up Hotel Street after

a long night shift at Shop 17 (sheet metal). It was about nine in the morning. At a few establishments along the street, sailors and soldiers were lined up. I said to my seat buddy, "I didn't know movies opened so early in Hawaii." He smiled at my naiveté. "They're not lined up for movies," he said, laughing. "Those are whorehouses. And it's legal in Hawaii."

The price was three dollars for three minutes. If you weren't finished by then, there would be a knock on the door and a burly bouncer would "suggest" that your time was up.

But that rarely happened, according to some of the madams. Most of the young men there were anticipating their first sexual experience. Usually, they were finished in seconds. Some, before they even started.

In the prostitution areas along Hotel and River streets were a number of prophylactic stations run by the military. After a visit to houses of prostitution, men were advised to go to a station for treatment against venereal disease. There they received a shot of penicillin, a new miracle drug.

Many of the madams became quite wealthy. Before the war ended, so did legal prostitution, but some stayed in Hawaii, putting their money into legitimate businesses, especially real estate. Others married well and eventually became respected, leading citizens in the community. Few knew their real story.

This was the beginning of my Hawaii adventure, one that's lasted for more than 60 years. In my wildest dreams, I never imagined that I would become a confidant of Marlon Brando, do charity work with Elvis Presley and get to know a very revealing side of Frank Sinatra—all because Hawaii was (and still is) Hollywood's favorite escape to Paradise.

In Hawaii, finally, I was in the right place at the right time.

By the time I arrived in Hawaii at age 18, I had already made up my mind about my future. I wasn't going to stay in sheet metal—I wanted to be a radio announcer. But back in the early '40s, radio in Hawaii was a vastly different industry than it is now. Radio in those days was what TV is to people today. The only difference was that instead of watching, we listened—and let the theater of the mind do the rest.

Most of the programs were network-originated. The local stations mostly just delivered the news, and announcers voiced the commercials. There were no Island radio personalities as we know them today. Only newscasters were allowed to inject their own names over the air: "This is so-and-so, and now the news."

There were only two Hawaii stations on the air then—KGMB (the CBS outlet) and KGU (an NBC station). I chose to audition at KGMB, where Owen Cunningham was the station manager. A prim, bald, middle-aged, mustachioed gentleman with a precise, deliberate speech pattern, Owen let me read a commercial and a short bit of news, then took me into his office.

"What part of Boston are you from?" he asked. I felt like I'd been hit square in the jaw.

"How'd you know I was from Boston?"

"It's your accent," he said.

"Accent?" I blurted. "Nobody's ever told me I had an accent!" I thought I talked like everyone else. This guy Cunningham must be nuts!

"Just what is a Boston accent?" I asked.

Kind, gracious Owen explained, then noted that announcers weren't hired if they any kind of a regional accent. I was so disappointed. My dream seemed to have collapsed right then and there. I had never anticipated anything like this.

"What can I do?" I sighed, almost in tears. Owen assured me that all was not lost. There was still hope. He suggested I study radio and speech. Find a good school—maybe in California, since there were none in Hawaii then. With study and hard work, he advised, I could lose my Boston accent.

In 1944 I arranged to be transferred from Pearl Harbor to the big Navy shipyard in Long Beach, California. I had learned that a new radio school had opened in Pasadena, and I enrolled. Home was a rented room in a South Pasadena boarding house. Fortunately, some of the men in residence also worked at the shipyard 30 miles distant, so there was always convenient transportation. I went to school three nights a week.

My instructor was Reed Browning, a young man who worked for NBC in Hollywood. Reed was kind, sympathetic and encouraging. I told him about my audition in Hawaii. He assured me that my Boston accent would eventually vanish. He was a fine teacher, and he couldn't have had a more willing or eager student.

Occasionally, Reed invited his students to the NBC studios to watch broadcasts and meet some of the announcers. That was a thrilling experience for me. A year later I graduated from the Pasadena Institute for Radio and immediately made arrangements to transfer back to Pearl Harbor, ready to conquer the Hawaii radio scene.

Soon after the war ended, I auditioned once again at KGMB. Owen Cunningham was still in charge, but this audition was vastly different than my earlier one. More than 50 young men showed up, most of them servicemen about to be discharged.

We gathered in the vast studio that KGMB used for live broadcasts. Behind the stage was a glass-enclosed technical booth. Each prospect was given a short newscast and a commercial to read.

As the audition progressed, I became more and more discouraged. Each man sounded like a network announcer. They were excellent. In my heart I knew I was way out of my league.

Two weeks later I received a letter from Owen Cunningham. I knew it was my rejection. Sadly, I opened it up.

To my shock and surprise I read that I had been selected as staff announcer at KGMB. Report to work immediately!

I couldn't believe it! Was this really true?

I called KGMB. It wasn't a joke. I had won the audition. I just had to know how I was picked, so I went to Owen's office. He explained: "Eddie, you must be aware that most of the men who auditioned for the job were experienced radio announcers before being inducted into the service. If I had hired any one of them, he'd probably stay in Hawaii just a short time and then leave to pursue a career on the Mainland. We're just a small radio station way out in the Pacific.

What we need is someone who has a lot of ambition, is willing to learn, and would do almost anything asked of him—and who wouldn't ask for a big salary. You're that person!"

The year was 1945. After my initial euphoria over breaking into radio, in reality it was quite boring. There were long shifts of just sitting at the board, or console—spinning records, giving station breaks and reading commercials. Honolulu definitely wasn't Los Angeles or New York. The action was in those major cities. We were the boondocks. Hicksville, USA. But we also had the great weather, beautiful beaches and gentle trade winds.

A radio career? Hardly. That's not to say we didn't have any local radio stars. A few Hawaii personalities made a very respectable living in those days.

Hal Lewis, for instance, was Hawaii's biggest radio personality. He had bounced around the dial a bit before landing a morning show that established him as the highest paid radio star ever in the Islands.

He adopted the name of J. Akuhead Pupule; loosely translated, that meant Crazy Fish Head. A former professional violinist blessed with a rich voice, a sharp sense of humor and the ability to pick the right music for the times, "Aku" was quite intelligent. Handsome he was not. He had his big nose trimmed. It didn't help.

Aku cut a wide swath in local society, becoming the most listened-to disc jockey in the Islands and at one time reportedly earning over one million dollars a year.

He had first arrived in Hawaii as a fiddler in the ship's orchestra on the *Lurline*. Once he became an Island resident, he never returned to his former life. He had a flock of children and a devoted wife.

Aku fancied himself a better golfer than he actually was. After finishing his long daily broadcasting stint from 5 to 10 a.m., he'd head for the Waialae Country Club where the golf sharpies were waiting for him. The betting was heavy. Over the years they cleaned his pockets of a small fortune.

Aku's radio stunts were legendary. One was his announcement that a downtown bank was giving two hundred dollars away. Hundreds of the curious showed up. Few were in line at first because they thought it was some sort of a joke. But when the bank actually started handing out the money, the lines circled the block and interrupted traffic.

He once announced an exciting parade in downtown Honolulu and listeners rushed down to see the activity. But Aku had made the whole thing up.

He was totally irreverent as he attacked Hawaii's political sacred cows. Most listeners loved him. Some despised him. But they all tuned in. His ratings were head and shoulders above the competition.

In 1947 I left KGMB to join Aku at KGU, the NBC station. As an additional source of income, I also decided to put together a small entertainment troupe, booking shows into nightclubs and the many military clubs on the island of Oahu. These service clubs were much more attractive to play than their civilian counterparts.

Aku was my star attraction, along with some novelty acts, a magician and a banjo player. I was the emcee and did a pantomime act—impersonating stars like Al Jolson and Jimmy Durante, mouthing the words while one of their records played in the background. Eventually, I added more and more comedy material. The pantomime act took a back seat and I finally retired the bit.

During a long shipping strike that nearly crippled Hawaii in 1949, I decided to try my luck as a stand-up comic on the Mainland. By then I had appeared in most of the clubs in Honolulu and thought I had enough material to strike out for the big time.

After a few months of managing only a few meager bookings in Los Angeles, I returned to my hometown of Boston. There, for the next five years, I worked small nightclubs all over New England. It was a difficult existence.

My best friend in those days was a young comedian-singer. His real name was Goro Suzuki, but he used an alias that sounded Chinese. Goro, who stood a slim 6' 2", was married to a beautiful, statuesque blonde. They had two boys. Those days, they were an unusual couple for staid New England and always drew double takes when together. Oriental men and beautiful Caucasian ladies as a couple were a rare sight at the time.

As a comic, he was very funny. Offstage, Goro was taciturn and withdrawn most of the time and often bitter about the world in general. Maybe it was because as a young man, he and his family were sent to an internment camp during the war, even though he was an American born and raised in San Francisco.

Although he had the most menacing appearance, in reality he was a pussycat. I sensed there was something very special about him, and we became fast friends.

One memorable event: I was booked for a week at a club in Pittsfield, Massachusetts, which was about a hundred miles or so from Boston, right on the New York state border. Suzuki had an emcee deal at a club close by. So we drove to Pittsfield together.

One night after my show, I was sipping a Coke at the bar before going to Goro's club to catch his last performance and drive him back to the hotel. The female singer in the show (a cute grandmother) was also sitting at the bar a few seats away, waiting for her ride, when the band's sax man approached her and tried to make conversation. He'd had a few drinks and was a bit obnoxious. She obviously didn't want to be bothered and told him so, but he persisted.

I intervened and suggested he leave her alone. This burly guy slid off his seat and menacingly staggered toward me. I was readying a kick to the groin when a blur shot past me, tackling the musician—almost bending the guy in two. It was the club manager. He waved a finger under the musician's nose, telling him in no uncertain terms to take his personal problems elsewhere.

I quickly left for Goro's club. While sitting at a table explaining to Suzuki what had happened at my club, in walked the inebriated musician. Spotting me, he moved threateningly towards me, spewing a string of epithets. Suzuki stood up, grabbed the musician's jacket, pulled his face to his and snarled menacingly, à la Humphrey Bogart.

"If you wanna whack Sherman, you better take care of me first," said Goro.

The blood drained from the guy's face. He backed off and slunk out of the club. Suzuki's act scared the hell out of him, as did his tough-looking Oriental face. For all the villain knew, Suzuki was some kind of judo or martial arts expert.

For the rest of that Pittsfield nightclub engagement, there was no more trouble from the musician. Goro later admitted that he was very frightened himself and almost soiled his underwear during that episode. Thank goodness, the tough-guy shtick worked and saved me from a possible hospital stay.

During my five years of criss-crossing New England, playing in numerous small nightclubs, most entertainers were employed usually for weekends or sometimes a week's engagement, if they got lucky.

I finally landed a "steady" gig in Boston's then very popular College Inn. It was the *Cage Aux Folles* of its day. Sold out nightly. Reservations were hard to get. What was the attraction? It was considered a gay club. The main attractions were the female "drag queen" impersonators. Still, half the show consisted of straight performers, meaning singers, novelty acts and so on. Basically, it was just a large revue.

The club was very plush. It had a strict dress code: coat and tie for men, dresses for women. Rocky Paladino and some "partners" owned the club. (Paladino was reputed to be the Mafia's number-one boss in New England.)

When word got out that the show was looking for a new emcee, I applied. Happily, I won the audition. At last, a steady job! But first, a two-week tryout.

My "dressing room" was a small corner with the impersonators. They were merciless in ridiculing me backstage. It was mostly friendly; however, some of the "girls" objected to my material, which consisted of making fun of what it was like working with gay people, as well as, of course, poking fun at myself.

For example: my opening line usually was—"I know what you're thinking: that I'm one of 'those.' Actually, folks, I'm one of the few normal people in this whole show. I happen to be very happily married. And I'd like to have you meet my wife."

Pointing to a male in the audience, I'd smile and say, "Harry, would you please stand up?"

After my two-week probation period, I signed a year's contract. For me this was a major coup. No more one-night stands. I had a regular job. Two shows a night. No more traveling!

As time went on, the "girls" became friendlier, and some began to confide in me about their lives and problems. I learned about a lifestyle I never knew existed. It was quite an education. They shared their world of being discriminated against, of being social outcasts.

My steady job came to an abrupt halt a year later, after Boston's powerful Archbishop Cardinal Cushing wrote a blistering editorial for Boston's top newspaper, castigating the Boston nightclubs he considered to be in bad taste and not suited for patronage.

The College Inn was at the top of his list.

By today's standards, the club actually would be considered quite tame. The show was, in reality, quite tasteful and entertaining. There was nothing that could be considered, in my view, off color.

Rocky immediately called a meeting of all employees. He told everybody that since he and his wife were big contributors to the church, and because Cushing did not think his club was fit for the general public, he had decided to close the premises and sell the establishment.

He called me aside and gave me a special gift. "I want you to know that I appreciate your work here," said Rocky. He patted me on the back, and then added, "If you think it will help, you have my permission to use my name anytime if you ever get in a jam. You never know..."

During my year at the College Inn, I had become friendly with Norm Crosby, who often visited the club. He and I came from the same neighborhood: Dorchester. Norm wanted to be a professional comedian and worked at comedy in his spare time, performing one-nighters wherever he could land a gig.

At the time, he was doing public relations for a business. He wanted to be in show biz full time. He often suggested we team up. I laughed and said, "What, and give up a regular job?"

After the College Inn closed, Norm and I did team up. We played a few engagements here and there, to mild success, while we tried out all sorts of material we swiped from other comedy teams. We tried different routines to find out what worked and what didn't.

Once, Norm and I were booked in an upscale hotel in Maine. We felt this engagement might lead to better jobs. Our routine went something like this: I opened and did about twenty-five minutes of comedy. Then I introduced Norm, and he did the same. After that, we collaborated on some stock comedy team material, and that was it.

This one particular night, Norm faced an unresponsive audience. He could hardly get them to laugh. For some reason, they had been okay for me, but not Norm. After the show in the dressing room, I asked Norm why he didn't bring me back for some double bits since he was bombing. He looked at me quizzically.

"Are you serious, Eddie? I was killing them," he said. "I had the crowd in the palm of my hand."

He then unbuttoned his shirt. "Look," he said, "I had this thing turned on all the way up." Wrapped around his stomach was some sort of hearing equipment.

"What's that?" I asked.

"During the war, I was in the Navy and a big gun went off near where I was standing and blew both my ears out. I'm practically deaf," Norm explained.

That night, we decided we should forget about being a comedy team. I believed Norm's "handicap" would prevent him from being successful in show business. Without hearing the audience reaction, his comedy and his timing would be affected. I strongly suggested to him that he forget about being a comedian and stick to public relations. I was sure he would be better off.

When I told this story to friends years later, after Norm established himself as a major comedy star, they would ask, "So what did Norm say to that?"

My answer? "He didn't hear me!"

I've never been so wrong about anything in my life. Norm continued playing second-rate clubs for many years, then slowly climbed out of the joints. He eventually developed a unique act, and this landed him a very coveted engagement: the opening act for Tom Jones at a time when the singer was the hottest attraction in the world. They toured together for a long time.

Norm became a solid national nightclub comedy star with his malapropisms. He played the top clubs coast-to-coast, TV shows, conventions and special functions for top dollar, and continues doing so today. He lives in Beverly Hills with his family, is financially secure and continues to be a major comedy attraction.

Not long ago, Norm sailed into Honolulu on a cruise ship, where he was the star entertainer. We had a reunion of sorts after not having any contact for years. We had a great time reminiscing about the old days and catching up. He has really made it in one of the most difficult of professions. I'm so proud of him, knowing what a struggle it was for him to reach the top. He couldn't be more deserving.

I didn't know it at the time, but I was heading for my last nightclub engagement in New England. I was driving from Boston to Albany, New York, to fill in for a cancelled comedian at a club called Ponzie's.

It was a dark and stormy night. The rain was coming down so hard, it was difficult to see the white line that divided the highway. Fortunately, there was hardly any traffic. Lightning and thunder split the skies. The whipping winds uprooted trees and littered the road. The radio warned that a major hurricane was in progress, and drivers were advised to get off the roads. I didn't listen to that advice, of course. I had a gig to go to.

Eventually, after a nine-hour drive, without stopping for food or rest, I arrived at my destination. A barely visible blinking neon sign in the window spelled out the club's name in a run-down, slummy section of the city. I was exhausted, hungry and without a hotel room.

After entering the dingy establishment, I asked for the manager. A short, stocky, beer-barrel type appeared, smelling of booze. He had half a cigar stuck in his mouth; a few wisps of hair covered his bald, bowling ball-shaped head. He grabbed my arm in a vice-like grip.

"You da new emcee?" he grunted. I nodded.

"Den, go to da bar and make my drunk customers laugh."

Surveying the scene, I was ready to retch. This was the dump of dumps. The bar was littered with some of the mangiest, most derelict types I had ever seen.

I walked over to the club boss and asked him for fifty dollars.

"What for?" he grunted.

"Gas for my car. I'm not working for you or in this shithouse. I'm going back to Boston."

"And if I don't give you the money?" he growled.

"Then I'm calling my manager, Rocky Paladino, right now, and I promise after I tell him you roughed me up, it will cost you a lot more than fifty dollars."

Apparently, that got the cockroach's attention. Rocky's name worked magic. He quickly came up with the money, and I was on my way. Another nine hours later through the vicious storm, I was back in Boston, exhausted. To be honest, I don't know how I ever made it back in one piece.

The next day, I was in my agent's office. I told him I was quitting this life. I'd had enough.

"What will you do?" he asked.

I smiled.

"I'm going home," I said. "To Hawaii. Thanks for everything. *Aloooooooha!*"

When I returned to Honolulu in 1955, KGU Radio hired me once again as a staff announcer. I was so happy to be home, I would have settled for picking up seashells on the beach for a living. However, it wasn't long before I was back in Honolulu's nightclub scene again, with another troupe of performers. It was radio during the day and show biz at night!

Honolulu's clubs then were mostly strip joints. However, the military bases had first-class nightclubs. The best. Working the military circuit three or four nights a week, I found myself earning much more than my radio salary. I also began booking Mainland acts into the clubs.

Meanwhile, Aku was getting even bigger on the local radio scene. Here's a story that's never been printed, and few know: Buck Buchwach, who eventually rose to become editor at the *Honolulu Advertiser*, had taken a five-year hiatus from the newspaper to open his own public relations firm. During that period, he had a business venture with Lewis that apparently soured.

One early morning, Aku showed up at Buck's residence. They got into an argument. Aku apparently lost his temper and went ballistic. He pulled out a gun and pointed it at Buck, threatening to kill him.

Buck went to the paper and wrote the story. It was *this* close to being the next day's headline. However, after further deliberation, it was decided that the best course of action was to do nothing about the episode in public. However, the two former friends never spoke to each other again, and Aku regularly attacked the *Advertiser* after that.

Ed Sheehan was another well-known local radio personality of the day. Ed and I had much more in common than just the same initials. He had come to Hawaii from Malden, Massachusetts, while I was from Dorchester, another section of Boston. We two Beantowners had both worked at Pearl Harbor, and we connected once again when we were both staff announcers at KGMB. We were like calabash cousins.

Ed was quite a character, especially in his youth through middle age. A real original—and an excellent writer. He would often disappear, getting blind drunk and eventually surfacing in the strangest places. A real Bohemian. Eventually, he married his Sally, who brought him to heel and made sure his wild days were over. Well, almost.

For many years Ed hosted an afternoon radio show called "Pauhana Concert" on KGU, upstairs in the News Building, where the *Advertiser* was published.

One afternoon, a friend of mine who happened to be a prostitute visited me in my office at the paper. She was a real Irma La Douce type—basically a very sweet young lady. She loved to come to the newspaper and gossip, telling me spicy stories about her life in the world's oldest profession.

That day I had an idea and asked her if she'd go along with a gag.

Would she go upstairs to the KGU studio and "visit" with Ed Sheehan? I would make a bet with him: that he couldn't finish reading a radio commercial while she was under his desk performing oral sex.

She thought it would be fun and agreed to play along. I called Ed. We made the bet—$10.

Up she went and I turned on the radio. Before long I heard Ed reading a car commercial.

"And so," he intoned, "if you want a great deal on an automobile, stop by Aloha Motors and"—he suddenly screamed—"buyyyyyyyy-eeeeeeee a carrrrrrrrr..."

I fell on the floor.

I won the bet.

Because KGU was on the top floor of the News Building, the home of the *Advertiser*, I would often visit the radio station after our military shows, then drop down to the second floor while the paper was being readied to go to press. For me, it was the most exciting place to be: reporters scrambling to finish their stories for the first edition, teletypes clacking madly away, people yelling and running all over the city room! It was wild. I loved it. What action!

When the first editions finally started rolling off the presses, Buck grabbed a couple papers and off we'd go to Kau Kau Korner to eat, gossip and read the paper. On the side, as a diversion, Buck wrote a weekly show-biz column titled "Kimo Kalahan." Many of the stories I told him about Honolulu after dark were used as material for his column.

Eventually, Buck suggested I try writing down the items I would tell him. I confessed I'd never written anything before. He convinced me to try, and said he'd edit and coach me. He added that his city editor duties kept him too busy to write about show biz.

I started with a weekly column titled "Backstage." The pay was thirty-five cents an inch, or about five dollars a column. It seemed to work. Then Buck asked me to do twice-weekly columns, then a column three times a week. I finally told him there just weren't enough items about show biz for three columns. He then suggested I include items of all kinds—human-interest stuff—about Hawaii.

Now my name headed the column, which ran from the top of the page to the bottom (about a thousand words). And the column ran on the third page, which was a highly coveted position.

The local press had never had the kind of column I was writing. I employed the three-dot style in the tradition of the great Walter Winchell. I injected the slang of show biz, twisted words around, used their phonetic spellings—"laffs," "thots"—and invented new words and phrases that were easily understood in Hawaii: Poi-pourri, Mynah Matters, Pali Periscope, Diamond Head-lines, Oh My Papaya, Hawaiian Eye-Openers, Coconut Milkshake, Pounding The Poi Beat, Lanai Lookout, Tropic Topics, The Poi Belt, Hulapaloozas, Lei Away Plan, Babes in Poiland, Honolulu Almanac, Luauland Lulu's, Sandwich Isle Spread, Sashimi Notes, Haolewood, Imu Whispers.

Many of the established journalists in town ridiculed and scoffed at my work. I realized they were envious, but I couldn't understand why. In my mind, I wasn't even in the same class as my critics; these other writers and reporters were smart, college educated. So why were they putting me down?

The snide remarks and minor backstabbing only increased after the paper surveyed its readers. *Advertiser* subscribers were asked to name their favorite features in the paper. Ann Landers, the syndicated advice columnist, was number one. What surprised everyone was number two. Me! (And number one among the local features.)

Soon, I was adding other ventures to my daily routine: radio shows, TV celebrity interviews, emceeing events of all kinds, speaking engagements. Plus a nonstop social life.

I also found that, thanks to my column, I had access to the many celebrities who came to town to work or play. The big-name actors and singers and athletes vacationed in the Islands for all the usual reasons—the beautiful scenery, the balmy weather, the friendly people, the fun and games. But, as it still does today, Hawaii held another carrot for the rich and famous. In the Islands, people generally leave them alone—no screaming crowds, no shouting paparazzi. For the most part, our islanders give celebrities their space, and the celebrities respond in kind—letting their hair down and relaxing in peace. And in my capacity as Hawaii's resident three-dot columnist, I had many opportunities to pal around with these famous folks—often as an interviewer, sometimes as a tour guide, sometimes as a confidant, many times as a friend.

So my career was off and running. A whole new world opened up for me! I had an office and a secretary. The phone never stopped ringing. A parade of people trooped in and out of my office all day long. Invitations poured in from folks in every walk of life. I was running a mile a minute—here, there and everywhere! Businessmen invited me to lunches. Politicians became my friends. Restaurants invited me to dinners.

It was like a three-ring circus.

This was better than show business. It was the most exciting time of my life. I was reborn. Of course, financially speaking, I was barely eking out a living. The *Advertiser* was struggling, and dollars were scarce. But I had found my calling.

I was a newspaper columnist.

THREE

Arthur Godfrey

For much of the 1950s and '60s, Arthur Godfrey was the biggest radio and TV star in America. You could add up all of today's radio talk show ratings, and the total would still pale in comparison to his tremendous drawing power.

Basically, Godfrey was a freckled-faced, ukulele-playing host and pitchman with an infectious chuckle, an unruly shock of red hair and a folksy, intimate delivery that made people feel like he was talking just to them. He seldom read from a script.

During his heyday, he was also one of the highest-paid entertainers in the country, armed with an "average man" approach and a sophistication that charmed the country. He kidded his sponsors and, above all else, was a master salesman. When he recommended a product, people purchased it. Naturally, advertisers loved him.

Godfrey loved to sing and play Hawaiian tunes on his uke. As a result, Hawaii received a fortune in national promotion and publicity from his radio and TV programs. He was an unpaid one-man advertising firm for Hawaii, giving the Islands more free publicity and promotion than a hundred visitors' bureaus put together!

Godfrey first fell in love with Hawaii when he came through the Islands during World War II. Then a lonely, unknown war correspondent, he was befriended by Kathleen Perry of the famed restaurant The Willows and he never forgot the unexpected aloha and Hawaiian hospitality he received.

"I learned a lot at Kathleen's Willows," he recalled. "She taught me to eat sashimi, opihi, laulau and all these other dishes that are so much better than many foods we eat on the Mainland."

In August 1959, shortly after Hawaii achieved statehood, Godfrey told me: "I'm afraid [Hawaii is] going to be another Miami Beach if you aren't careful. They built hotels in Miami until there wasn't room for any more, and now they're half full. The place where you can enjoy Hawaiiana is getting smaller and smaller. But, even that little bit is heaven, and I love it."

It was as though he had peeked into a crystal ball.

"I love these islands, this state and all things Hawaiian," he told me. "I have probably contributed as much as anyone to her ultimate destruction. Hawaii isn't ready, but the tidal wave of tourism has already broken on Waikiki Beach. Visitors are sure to destroy the things they come here to seek. Like all others who deeply love this place, I'm brokenhearted over it."

Godfrey was here to do a series of shows from the lawn of the Royal Hawaiian Hotel. He told me he wanted to start his TV show with a long shot of Duke Kahanamoku coming in on a wave.

After he asked Duke, however, the legendary surfer and champion swimmer just shook his head. "No can do, Artur.'" (That's how he pronounced Arthur's name.) "Hafta go Mainland. Maybe some other time."

Godfrey was taken aback. "Duke, I don't come here every day," he said. "Millions will be seeing you!"

Duke just shrugged his shoulders. "No can. Maybe next time."

Not many people would turn down such an opportunity for national exposure. Then again, there was only one Duke. He couldn't care less about national acclaim. He had it. Been there, done that—and then some.

I accompanied Godfrey on many of his Hawaiian adventures. Once, in a pineapple field, he personally picked a ripe pineapple, sliced it and took a few juicy bites. He said, "I've been telling people [on radio and TV] that the taste of a freshly picked pineapple is worth the entire trip to Hawaii."

On another occasion, Godfrey, perhaps the highest-priced pilot in the world, flew me to the island of Molokai. Aloha Airlines had provided Godfrey with a charter DC-3. He took a day off after recording his radio and TV shows, and invited some of his cast and crew along for the ride.

I joined Godfrey and Captain Harry Saunders in the cockpit as we winged past Diamond Head. "How many hours do you have in the air?" I asked him.

"Been flying for thirty-five years, my boy, and at the moment I have about 8,600 hours. Last time I was in Hawaii, I flew with Harry to Molokai. I had more [flight] hours than he had."

Godfrey detoured from the regular route, taking instead several scenic paths that went beyond the normal tourist flight. Charlie Andrews, Godfrey's show producer, apparently had full confidence in his star's piloting ability. He slept through the whole thing!

Harry Larson, who ran Libby's pineapple plantation on Molokai, had three cars waiting for us. Soon after we landed, we were on the way to Larsons' weekend home.

Our caravan stopped briefly at Maunaloa Plantation on the west end of the island so we could wash up and rest. Godfrey lay down on a couch and fell sound asleep almost instantly. A half-hour later, we were again on our way.

On the way to the Larson abode, Godfrey paused when he noticed an interesting woman tending to her cows at Kamiloloa. He got out of the car and walked over to shake hands with Mrs. Naehua, who, with her husband, owned a small ranch. Godfrey, himself a farm owner, looked over the cattle. Mrs. Naehua handed him two loaves of bread that she had baked that morning.

The Larson home on the east end of Molokai had a festive air. Luau torches were blazing, and dozens of the longest and thickest leis had been flown in from Maui.

After the repast, Godfrey lit up a huge cigar.

"Kamehameha never had it so good," he laughed.

For younger generations who may not know of Arthur Godfrey, here's a little peek at his background: Godfrey served in the Navy for four years, then enlisted in the Coast Guard for another three. (I think he and I got a little friendlier when he learned that I also spent time in the Coast Guard.)

During the Depression years, he was doing well in radio in the Washington, D.C., area. A violent car crash, however, nearly took his life. He was hospitalized for months. Listening closely to radio then, he realized that the stiff formal announcers of that day couldn't connect to the average listener. They spoke as if to a crowd, not one person. When Godfrey got well and returned to the airwaves, he affected a new style.

His speech was relaxed and informal, as if he were just talking directly to you, friend to friend. He did his commercials the same way. In no time, this unusual style of intimate broadcasting made him the biggest regional star of his day.

His affable personality combined warmth, heart and bits of double-entendre repartee that earned him adulation from all sorts of fans who felt he was personally talking just to them.

Behind Godfrey's on-air warmth, however, was a cold, controlling personality. It was reported that in staff meetings he could be abusive and intimidating. He brought in big profits to the network and was respected professionally. However, behind the scenes, it was said that many of the network executives he worked for were not very fond of him.

Despite his great success in radio and television, Godfrey had problems with the media. He involved himself in public feuds with some of New York's most powerful newspaper columnists, and the media began running exposé articles on Godfrey, linking him to several members of his female entertainment gang.

Be that as it may, nothing could change Hawaii's love and adulation for Arthur Godfrey. He was the Island's greatest booster and number-one publicity machine. He had fallen in love with Hawaii right from the beginning, and this never diminished.

In the early 1960s, he began experiencing chest pains. It was cancer. One of his lungs was removed. After radiation treatments, Godfrey beat the substantial odds against him. When he finally returned to work, however, it was minus his two biggest TV programs, *Arthur Godfrey Time* and *Arthur Godfrey and His Friends*. Only his radio show remained.

Slowly, his public image began to fade, despite occasional mini-comebacks. By the 1980s, emphysema had become a problem. He battled but couldn't beat the disease. He died in 1983 and is buried not far from his farm in Leesburg, Virginia.

He had an incredible life.

Fast Fact: Arthur Godfrey

In 2001, Arthur Godfrey was inducted into the Ukulele Hall of Fame Museum in Duxbury, Massachusetts. The museum's inaugural inductee (in 1996) was King David Kalakaua, Hawaii's "Merrie Monarch."

FOUR

Albert Finney

The year was 1963. Albert Finney had just finished an energetic Tahitian dance with the Puka Puka Otea girls at Queen's Surf, then one of Waikiki's premier nightclubs near the famed Natatorium. He plopped into his chair, slightly out of breath, and lit a cigarette. At the time, few in the audience recognized this young (he was twenty-six then), good-looking "tourist" with sandy hair and no real distinguishing facial characteristics.

In fact, Finney was just about the hottest new male star in films. He had recently made a film called *Tom Jones*, and it scored amazing box office numbers. All sorts of awards were being flung at the movie, and even more offers were pouring in for Finney, who basically was a British stage actor devoted to the works of Shakespeare. This sudden international fame that resulted from *Tom Jones* actually freaked the actor out.

One of the funniest and most talked-about scenes in the film involved Tom Jones (Finney) and one of his many women sitting across from each other, eating dinner at an inn. In the scene, they begin seducing each other in an overtly sexual manner, licking lips, gnawing on chicken legs and making bedroom eyes. It has to be seen to be appreciated, but trust me, it was hilarious!

Throughout his acting career, Finney has impressed critics with his ability to step into a role and wear a character's persona no matter what age, nationality or avocation. In his more than forty years of film acting, he portrayed a Polish Pope, a Belgian detective, an Irish gangster, a British miser, an American lawyer, a Scottish king, a

German religious reformer and a Roman warrior—all with convincing authenticity.

And that was just in films. His first love was always the stage.

Sitting with me at Queen's Surf that night, Finney spoke his mind about his career. "Frankly, I'm running away from all that nonsense of being a movie star," he said. "I just don't want any part of it. Being a film star scares me a bit. Luckily, I'm not well known at the moment, which enables me to have the freedom of movement I want.

"Oh, I realize that when one gets famous, there is a public responsibility. But I don't quite know how to handle it. Basically, I'm a stage actor and have been earning my living on the stage since I was nineteen. People don't usually bother stage actors, but it's different in films. Right now I just want to travel anywhere in the world I want. I want to see places and people. I don't want to be tied down with commitments. If I knew I had a picture to do five months from now, I'd be worrying about the part and couldn't enjoy anything else."

After that night, Finney and I frequently closed a number of Waikiki clubs, and we became good friends. Originally, he only intended to stay in Honolulu for a few days. But, as happens so often, the Polynesian lifestyle infected him and he lengthened his Hawaii visit to a couple months. Even then, he was reluctant to leave, and he returned a number of times over the years.

Finney was nominated for Best Actor honors for *Tom Jones*. He called and asked me what I was doing the night of the Oscars. "Just gonna watch the show," I said.

"Then how about joining me? I've got some birds (girls) I'm taking out on a catamaran." I told him I'd go only if I could bring a radio along so I could listen to the Academy Awards. *If he wins*, I figured, *I'll have me a nice scoop.*

Finney agreed. He didn't care to see or hear the show. Just wanted to go sailing.

I found a nice spot on the tarpaulin above the deck of the catamaran to observe the action and listen to the Academy Awards. Finney was having a great time, tossing down the Polynesian drinks and dancing with his "birds."

Finally, "Best Actor" was announced. Sidney Poitier was the winner. When I yelled down the information to Finney, he stopped the dancing and asked everybody to raise their glasses in a deserved toast to a great actor: Sidney Poitier. That was class. Then the music started up again, and the dancing and fun continued.

It was dark by the time we sailed the cat back into Waikiki. A bunch of lights from shore hit the vessel. TV reporters were waiting. Finney asked me if I would talk to my contemporaries on his behalf. So I jumped off and said to them, "No story here. Sidney Poitier won for *Lilies of the Field*." But the reporters were persistent, and Finney reluctantly talked to them.

A few years later, I was in London on vacation. Honolulu media personality Ed Sheehan and his wife, Sally, went to London every year, where they rented a flat for months. So, while I was in London, we dined regularly and got the scoop about various shows and plays. One night, I learned we were all going to see the same play starring Albert Finney and Rachel Roberts.

Finney's character was a slovenly, middle-class British man. Of course, he was just brilliant. As we walked up the theater aisle after the show, we talked about how sensational he was. So I said to the Sheehans, "Let's go backstage and congratulate him on a magnificent performance."

Ed looked at me like I had lost my marbles. "Are you crazy?" he asked. "This is London. Nobody here knows who the hell you are. What makes you think you can even get backstage? Forget it. Please don't embarrass me." I told him I was going anyway, and he could join me if he wanted to. Ed was really upset, but he went along.

At the dimly lit stage door, a little old man let us in. I presented my card and asked if could have a word with Mr. Finney. The gentleman asked us to wait and excused himself. Ed and Sally fidgeted and hardly said a word.

Soon a door opened and Finney stuck his head out. "Eddie," he yelled, "is that really you?" He came racing out, grabbed me in a bear hug and danced me around. "How the hell are you? How long will you be here? When can we get together?"

I smiled. "Albert, please let me introduce my friends from Hawaii, Mr. and Mrs. Ed Sheehan." The look on their faces was priceless. They couldn't believe this was happening.

My little "surprise" worked to perfection, and the Sheehans have told this story over and over for many years. Me, too.

Fast Fact: Albert Finney

In order to star in the Academy Award-winning film *Tom Jones*, Albert Finney turned down the role of T.E. Lawrence in *Lawrence of Arabia*.

FIVE

Bette Midler

In the early 1960s, while my late wife Peggy Ryan was directing one of the many shows she did for Diamond Head Theatre, a local community theater company in East Honolulu, she told me about some difficulty she was having with one of her teenage performers. "She's a talented, sweet little girl," Peggy noted, "but quite difficult to direct. When everyone is dancing to the left, this girl goes to the right. She is so spirited, she just does what she pleases." Peggy asked me to attend one of her rehearsals, and that was when I met the girl and her mother. The kid obviously had talent and ambition. But so did many of the other young performers in the show. Nothing unusual.

Time would prove me wrong, of course. Bette Midler turned out to be quite special, indeed.

Bette was born and raised in Honolulu, where her father was a painter at Pearl Harbor and a tinkerer at home. Their backyard was full of junk that her father enjoyed working with. Sadly, he had absolutely no interest in his daughter's love of entertainment.

Because I was a columnist, the girl grilled me with questions about the rich and famous in the entertainment world. She wanted to know everything about everybody in show business. Her mother, Ruth, wanted to know if I thought her daughter had talent and a chance to make it. My best advice to Bette was that she should listen to Peggy, who knew show business inside and out. She had been there and done that.

"And," I told her, "never give up the dream."

When the movie *Hawaii*, starring Max von Sydow and Julie Andrews, was filmed on location in the Islands, Bette landed a part as an extra. Her one scene consisted of getting into a rowboat to go ashore. Playing a young missionary, she wore one of those "Mother Hubbard" costumes. She was barely recognizable.

For some reason, the scene could not be completed in Hawaii. As a result, Bette was invited to Hollywood, where the scene was finished. Then she made her decision. "New York, here I come."

Before she left Hawaii, I gave her a gentle warning. I told her about the thousands of ambitious, young and talented girls who go to New York every year dreaming of stardom. Most fail and eventually return home. I told her how difficult it would be, how great the odds were against success. I told her that many short, bosomy, Jewish girls like her from all around the country try to do the same thing every day. Few succeed.

Did she have talent? Of course she did. She sang a little, acted some. How good was she? Who really knew? Only time would tell. But no matter what, I cautioned her not to be disappointed, no matter what happened.

"Enjoy the experience," I advised her.

She and two friends teamed up for the upcoming trip. Her girlfriend, Lynn Ellen Hollinger (another aspiring young actress), and Bob Basso (who was just getting out of the Navy and was stationed in Hawaii) managed to put some bucks together for a second-hand car, and they all headed out to seek fame and fortune. (Dr. Basso, as we jokingly refer to him today because he has a Ph.D, has enjoyed a long and storied career as a TV newscaster, actor, director, author and motivational speaker. Even today, he likes to spin yarns about their cross-country odyssey.)

"I'll never forget the time we hit Las Vegas early one morning," Basso once wrote. "As we spied Caesar's Palace, Bette shouts, 'Stop the car!' She jumps out, looks up at the hotel's marquee and yells, 'Someday I'll be back here and will be the biggest star you've ever seen.'"

Against all odds, it happened.

In 1966, the *Honolulu Advertiser* sent me to New York to cover the movie premiere of *Hawaii*, a year after it was filmed. Before I left, Ruth Midler called and told me to be sure to visit her daughter, who was now playing a small role in a Broadway musical. I promised her I would.

After sitting through half of the movie, I left the theater to make my deadline and dashed to the United Press office to file my movie review. Then I hailed a taxi to the theater.

It was winter and snowing. I was freezing. I arrived at the stage door just as the show was breaking. The little girl from Hawaii, now twenty-one years old, emerged all bundled up. When she saw me, she let out a shriek. We hugged and headed for the nearest deli. We talked for hours. Bette filled me in on some of her New York experiences, her ups and downs. She told me how she pounded the pavement and did all sorts of odd jobs—from being a go-go dancer to doing children's theater—just for survival during her first few months in the Big Apple. She eventually won an audition to play the third daughter in the musical *Fiddler on the Roof*.

She was ecstatic about her life. "It's just so wonderful now," she told me. "Can you believe it? I'm getting known, meeting so many wonderful people. I've never been so happy."

About 2 a.m., I walked her to the subway station, we hugged and kissed, said aloha, and I wished her luck. She was going to make it. She *had* made it. But it was really just the beginning. Who knew how big she would eventually become?

A few years went by. Once again, I was visiting New York. The first show I saw on Broadway during this visit was a musical revue called *Clams on the Halfshell*. The theater was sold out for its entire run. The star of the show was my little girl from Hawaii—now the new theatrical darling of New York. The biggest star on Broadway: Bette Midler! Just the thought of it gave me chills. This little girl from Aiea was now the toast of Manhattan. Just unbelievable.

The large 2,000-seat Minskoff Theater was filled to capacity. When the curtain went up, there was a huge clamshell on stage. In the middle was the "pearl" (Bette) dressed in a cellophane-type grass skirt and bra, and draped in leis. That's how her revue started. I guess it was Bette making a statement of some sort. Like, "This is who I am, folks.

Not a sophisticated New Yorker, but really a simple little girl from a simple little place in the backwoods of Honolulu."

Bette's show was a knockout. A tour de force. She sang, she danced, she was hilarious. With her God-given megawatt personality, she swept the audience off its feet. In the end, everybody in the theater was standing and cheering—and screaming for more.

I was never so proud of anyone in my life. Tears were pouring down my cheeks. Bette had conquered the world.

It turned out that playing Tzeitel in *Fiddler* was the break she needed. It got Bette on her feet, gave her experience and a bit of security. Often, after the show, she and a *Fiddler* cast member would go to a small club called the Improv, a showcase for young talent who appeared without pay, hoping to be discovered. The club's owner, Budd Friedman, became her manager and was able to book her on a series of TV shows. Slowly, she was getting noticed. Still, she never neglected honing her talent. She never stopped studying. What little she could spare went for lessons in singing, dancing and acting. It was all part of her regular routine.

One day, Bette got a tip that the owner of the newly decorated Continental Baths planned to present entertainment on weekends, and they needed a singer. She quickly took the job.

Her salary was fifty dollars a night. The audience was mostly male homosexuals wrapped in bath towels. To say she dazzled her audience is putting it mildly. She was absolutely outrageous. Dressed like a wild young Carmen Miranda with a touch of Mae West—you'll have to look those names up, kiddies—she camped, strutted and displayed a bigger-than-life personality that hadn't been seen since the halcyon days of burlesque and vaudeville. She sang hits from the 1930s, '40s, '50s and '60s—novelty songs, blues and rock.

Suddenly, Bette was one of a kind. Even her accompanist was singled out as a special talent—a young musician named Barry Manilow. "We had been rehearsing for about a week," Manilow recalled. "Then [Bette] walked out with apples and fruit on her head, and was not the Bette I knew. She became the 'Divine Miss M.' I had never felt such electricity. I found myself laughing hysterically at her jokes, weeping at her ballads, and at the end I was on my feet like everybody else, cheering for her. I had never seen anything like it. Nobody else has to this day."

Barry and Bette worked together for the next three years. Slowly but surely, fame and success enveloped them both.

"During those struggling years I came to really get to know her," Manilow recalled. "Even then, her private life was very different than [her onstage personality]. She's actually very serious and bright—and quiet. I always felt she had the soul of a librarian."

Word quickly spread about this exciting, versatile, new performer taking New York by storm. Suddenly audiences, other than the usual bathhouse crowd, began to show up. Celebrities discovered Bette, and she became the "in" talent of the Great White Way. Offers for her services began to pour in. Johnny Carson signed her, and for the next two years she was a semi-regular on his show. Bette's career had skyrocketed. She was a national star.

That night, after the show at the Minskoff, her dressing room overflowed with the glitterati of New York—actors, agents, producers, media, politicians, etc.—all paying homage to Broadway's hottest new sensation.

Bette spied me across the room, flashed me the "shaka" sign (a Hawaiian greeting) and motioned for me to stay.

After the crowd finally dispersed, just a few members of her cast remained. A limo was waiting. Along the way, the stretch dropped off her cast members at various residences until only the two of us were left.

Bette directed the driver to a dimly lit restaurant. As we entered, one of her recordings was playing. Coincidence? It was all like one big movie scene.

We talked for hours. She was just as stunned as I was over her success. "Incredible, isn't it?" she remarked, shaking her head. "What a shame my father never saw my performances. He thought what I did was junk. He wasn't interested at all. I think he would have been happier if I were an opera singer or some other kind of professional."

This time, I didn't walk her to the subway station. Bette and the limo dropped me off at my hotel.

Since those days, Bette has enjoyed one of the most phenomenal show business careers in entertainment history. Even now, in her sixties, she remains a huge international star.

A few years ago, the local community honored me with a roast and toast. The show was held at the Hawaii Theatre in downtown Honolulu, with all proceeds going to charity.

A number of videos from various celebrities who couldn't make it in person were compiled for the event. I took a gamble and asked Bette's New York office months earlier if Bette could be one of the show's roasters. Hey, you never know if you don't ask.

Not hearing from her as show time was approaching, I figured, "Well, she's just too busy and has many more important things to do than schlep all the way to Hawaii just to say a few words about an old friend." Like all major celebrities, she's constantly bombarded with all kinds of requests. That just goes with the territory.

Guess what? Just before the roast started, a package arrived. It was a video from Bette. She delivered. People were bowled over by her speech.

Here it is in its entirety:

"Aloha everyone, and aloha especially to you, Eddie Sherman—one of the great lights of my life. I am very happy to count myself as one of your friends and I am very happy to be included in this celebration of your life and your work.

"When I was a little girl, reading Eddie Sherman's column every day was one of the highlights of my life. Eddie always made Honolulu seem like a hotbed of show business activity and intrigue. And, in fact, he was partly responsible for lighting a fire under me and forcing me off the island and into New York City.

"His writing was always exciting, excitable. He was always the kind of person who made you feel as if you were part of the experience of the Great White Way. I don't know how he managed to do it, because we were so far away from New York, but somehow he did. And so I'd like to say thank you, Eddie, for setting me off on my way, and thank you for the many, many years of great, great entertainment in print. I love you. Aloha."

Fast Fact: Bette Midler

Two of Bette Midler's hit singles—*Wind Beneath My Wings* (#44) and *The Rose* (#83)—were listed among the American Film Institute's "100 Years of the Greatest Songs" in 2004.

SIX

BOB HOPE

I have always been a Bob Hope fan. He was one of America's greatest laugh makers, a star from his days in vaudeville, on Broadway and through thousands of radio broadcasts, some seventy movies, hundreds of TV specials and Oscar-hosting gigs. He performed before millions of World War II troops all over the world. Without a doubt, Hope left a matchless legacy of laughter and joy.

He was a legend, an icon, and certainly one of the greatest entertainers of all time. So, at the risk of offending the Bob Hope fans who may be reading this, there was a side of Hope that was hardly ever publicized and few knew: Hope was a very shrewd, astute and extremely successful businessman.

For example, most of the United Service Organizations (USO) shows he did gratis were actually very financially rewarding for Hope. Yes, he did the shows for free. However, they were usually filmed, and television networks paid Hope a handsome remuneration for the right to air those shows on national TV.

Most of the costs of producing the shows were borne by the military, which supplied the transportation, accommodations, food and so forth. The entertainers who toured with Hope received minor remuneration. Result: the network had a free paid-for production, with Hope receiving a very substantial network salary. The deal was a gold mine for Hope and the network.

Another of Hope's quiet but very profitable sidelines was doing benefits for various institutions whenever there was an opening in his busy schedule. This particular vignette happened in Hawaii in the early 1960s, with one of his so-called "benefits":

A well-known Island hospital received a call one day from Hope's representative. The hospital was asked if they would be interested in having Bob Hope play a benefit for them. Naturally, the hospital was ecstatic and jumped at this great opportunity.

The hospital was told that Hope would be coming through Honolulu on his way home from a Japan trip and would be happy to stop over for the benefit show. The hospital was then informed of the terms: for doing this one-night performance, Hope would receive his regular $60,000 guarantee. Anything raised beyond that fee would belong to the hospital. (I know all this because the public relations person for the hospital gave me the whole story. She was involved with the project from the beginning.)

Naturally, everybody involved was thrilled. Those affiliated with the hospital worked feverishly selling tickets. Unfortunately, by the time of Hope's appearance, ticket sales were still thousands of dollars shy of Hope's $60,000 guarantee.

After the financially disastrous show, hospital officials informed Hope that if they gave him his guarantee as contracted they would lose thousands of dollars—money that they could not afford to lose.

Big hearted, generous Hope absolutely refused to negotiate, but charged them another $2,500 on top of the $60,000 guarantee because his wife, Delores, sang an unscheduled song. Who benefited? Hope, of course. The hospital was left deeper in the hole thanks to his "generosity."

Hope did hundreds of these "benefits" for many years all over the country as a side venture during his constant travels. It was an easy way to pick up some extra change. Many of these benefits ended up financial disasters like the Honolulu "benefit." These shows were hardly publicized.

The Honolulu hospital was just too embarrassed to say a word about the flop show and the financial hole they got into. They bit the bullet and licked their wounds. Of course, what the public knew about Hope were all his successes and great philanthropic generosity.

This is another example of why Hope was one of the wealthiest entertainers in history, and one of the most successful real estate moguls in Hollywood.

Thanks for the memories, Bob, and aloha!

Fast Fact: Bob Hope

Bob Hope entertained eleven U.S. presidents in his career, from FDR to Bill Clinton. He died on July 27, 2003, at 100 years of age.

SEVEN

Don Ho

In 1957, I was a bachelor and shared an apartment in Waikiki with Flash Miller, who managed the popular Queen's Surf nightclub. Flash asked me one day if I knew of someone who could replace his star attraction, Sterling Mossman, at the Barefoot Bar. Mossman was going on a two-week vacation.

I suggested myself. Naturally, Miller thought the idea was crazy. But I had a plan. I would basically take a page from Ed Sullivan, who at the time hosted the top variety show on television. Sullivan was a New York columnist, while I was a Hawaii columnist. He introduced people from the audience, and I would do the same thing. But we would have entertainers planted in the audience who would be our "guests," and they'd come up and do their bit when called upon.

Miller thought it was a great idea and not very expensive. He quickly went out and employed a band for the two-week period. The band was this group from Kaneohe led by a little-known performer named Don Ho.

Much to everyone's surprise, our show was an instant hit, and for two weeks the Barefoot Bar was packed.

One night during a guest's performance, Don and his band members were having a conversation behind the entertainer. I was furious. I told Don later how unprofessional and discourteous it was to the entertainer.

"Never do it again," I warned him, "or I'll see that you have a hard time getting another job in Waikiki."

He just shrugged. "Okay."

A few months later, Don was starring in Waikiki at Duke

Kahanamoku's. He was a roaring success.

Don eventually became the biggest entertainment name in Hawaii.

About our Barefoot Bar show, Ho quipped, "It had the worst emcee and the worst band. But we were a big hit."

What was, and is, so special about Don Ho? How did he become such a major attraction?

He's of medium height, and not particularly attractive. He mumbles. He appears to have hardly any energy and often performs like he's sleepwalking. He doesn't possess a particularly good voice. What is his big talent? Why is he so popular?

I've been watching him and writing about him for most of his professional life. I've seen hundreds of his performances. Yet, I'm still baffled at how he manages to capture an audience and weave his special magic. I've taken numerous guests to his shows over the years. After the first few minutes, they often ask me, "What's the big deal about this guy?" Then, two hours later, they're on their feet giving him a standing ovation.

My own opinion? His "magic" is sheer charisma. Don was born with it. He has that special magnetism, presence, personality and charm—and yes, incredible sex appeal. People just eat up his laid-back, "I-don't-give-a-damn" Polynesian attitude. Like he often says, "It ain't no big thing."

It's just magic, that's all.

Don's performance schedule these days includes stops at many of the Indian gambling casinos proliferating around the country. There are more than 400 of them coast-to-coast. And his shows are often sellouts. Asked why he's so popular on this circuit, he laughs and says, "They think I look like an Indian, so I must be one. People seem to believe that."

Don has always been one of Hawaii's most talked-about performers. When he first came to prominence in Waikiki, there were always rumors about his drinking, carousing and sexual activities. The youthful days of his Waikiki adventures were a bit on the wild side. His dressing room was always filled to capacity after shows with visiting young co-eds eager for a look, hug, kiss or even the ultimate Don Ho private favor.

Now in his mid-seventies, Don continues to tour the country, and many of these former co-eds, now gray-haired grandmas, still flock to his shows, reliving their happy Waikiki memories. For his part, Don still has a liquid-filled glass on his piano, and will take an occasional sip. But booze it ain't.

Recently, Don made headlines around the world when he had stem cells injected into his failing heart. The procedure seems to have helped. He's cut back on his schedule, but still performs one or two nights weekly.

Don will never retire as long as he can still walk out on a stage. Performing is his life. He can't live without it.

Fast Fact: Don Ho

Don Ho was a fighter pilot in the Air Force. He left the service in 1960 to tend to his ailing mother, and to perform at Honey's, her nightclub in Kaneohe.

EIGHT

Donald O'Connor and Rocky Marciano

It was the mid-1960s, and Donald O'Connor was in Honolulu for a week of concerts at Neal Blaisdell Center. That, of course, meant a big reunion with his former film partner, Peggy Ryan, who was my wife at the time. As a matter of fact, he even enlisted her in a "comeback" of sorts. So Peggy brought her tap shoes out of mothballs for the week's engagement, and the two teamed up for a special dance number that stopped the show. It was called "Me and My Shadow."

It went like this: Donald first sang the "Shadow" song. Then a huge screen came down behind him and as he danced, so did his "shadow" behind him. Every move he made, the shadow made. He wore a tux and hat. So did the shadow. Toward the end of the number, the shadow began to make some mistakes (on purpose), and then the audience realized it was somebody else behind the screen—not his shadow.

At the finish, the shadow came out from behind the screen, took a bow with Donald and removed its hat. The blond hair cascaded down, and Peggy was recognized. The applause was deafening. Once again, they were a hit.

The first time Peggy and Donald met was at the Hollywood Professional School. "He was in the fourth grade forever," recalled Peggy. "That's because he was always on the road, playing vaudeville with his family. When he'd come back, I was in a higher grade, but he'd still be in the fourth grade."

Peggy shared this story: "I was appearing at the Mansfield Theater in New York, and he was doing vaudeville with his family. He called and said, 'I got an audition across the way for a show called *Best*

Foot Forward. Let's do a number from *Meet the People* (the show Peggy was in at that time). We're a shoo-in!'

"So, here I am, already in a Broadway show and never had to do a real audition before. We show up for the audition and are given a number. When it's our turn, we go into our dance. Halfway through, somebody yells. 'All right. Next!' We really bombed. Here we were, doing well in our show business careers on Broadway, and we couldn't even pass an audition."

At the time Universal was looking for a young couple to give some competition to Judy Garland and Mickey Rooney, the biggest young stars at MGM. Their musicals were gold mines. Peggy and Donald were teamed with other young dancers for a film titled *The Jiving Jacks and Jills.*

"After the film's preview, they'd give out cards for the audience to fill out," recalled Peggy. "Apparently, we clicked with the film viewers. They wanted to know more about 'that dark-haired couple.'"

From 1942 to 1945, Peggy and Donald teamed up in more than a dozen musicals for Universal. "We worked one picture after another. It's amazing we had as much fun as we did, grinding them out like that," said Peggy.

The musicals ended when Donald was drafted into the Army. Throughout the remainder of World War II, Universal continued to release the very popular and profitable O'Connor-Ryan musical films it had rushed into production.

When Donald left the Army, Universal cast him in a non-dancing role in 1950 as a hapless Army private who couldn't convince anyone that he had a mule that could talk. *Francis the Talking Mule* was a big hit, and that began a successful run of *Francis* films. A couple years later, Donald was loaned out to MGM for what is regarded as his greatest film triumph: a co-starring role with Gene Kelly and Debbie Reynolds in the great classic, *Singin' in the Rain.*

If he never made another film, Donald would be a musical comedy immortal solely for the athletically uproarious "Make 'Em Laugh" number in *Singin' in the Rain*. Gene Kelly himself said it was one of the greatest tap numbers ever put on film.

Donald never forgot how the number came to be: "They didn't have a solo for me in the movie, and I couldn't think of anything," he recalled. "Just by chance, [composer-arranger] Roger Edens came in with this number, "Make 'Em Laugh." Kelly said to take a couple of girl assistants and see what I could come up with. So I started ad-libbing, doing pratfalls and whatever. And they laughed.

"I couldn't think of a finish, and then I remembered I had done the run-up-the-wall in two other pictures, so I added another wall and finished by going right through it. We filmed the whole sequence in a day. My body absorbed a lot of punishment. I was still sore three days later when I came back to work. Everybody on the set applauded me."

Donald laughed. "Then Gene came over. He asked if I could do the number all over again. I said sure, but why? He explained the cameraman accidentally fogged out all the film. After the sequence was completed, I was taken to the hospital—massive bruises and exhaustion."

For his Honolulu engagement, Donald leased a house on Kalanianaole Highway, right on the beach. He couldn't wait to get home after the show every evening and relax with a little libation. Yes, he was drinking then.

Like me, Donald was a big boxing fan. He boxed in the Army. He was fast and good. He learned the sport from his father and uncle when the family was on the carnival circuit. Donald was just a kid. His uncle would take on all comers. If they lasted a round, they won a prize.

If a particular customer showed he was a challenge, the uncle would move the opponent towards the painted backdrop of the ring behind which Donald's father was hiding with a baseball bat. Most of these customers never knew what hit them.

One night, after a few drinks, Donald started talking about boxing. He began by showing me how to throw a right hand, and then demonstrated various other types of punches.

An idea hatched. I challenged Donald to demonstrate the proper way to throw a right cross. I ended the discussion by saying, "Okay, Donald. Tomorrow I'm bringing over an expert who'll show you how

In 1945 I was a fledgling staff announcer for KGMB radio in Honolulu.

That's me (*bottom, fourth from right*) at age ten, playing football with the neighborhood kids in Boston. *Opposite*: My early Honolulu nightclub shows included various comedy bits and sometimes even a blackface turn as Al Jolson (here at Lau Yee Chai). *Left*: In "Ten Nights in a Barroom," a 1949 musical revue at the old Waikiki Tavern.

BILLY HOWELL

My sixth-grade teacher, Marjorie Ellis (*below right*), helped turn my life around. When she visited Honolulu years later, I gave her the grand tour, including a visit with Hickam Air Force Base Commanding General Hunter Harris. *Opposite*: Norm Crosby and I on tour on the New England nightclub circuit.

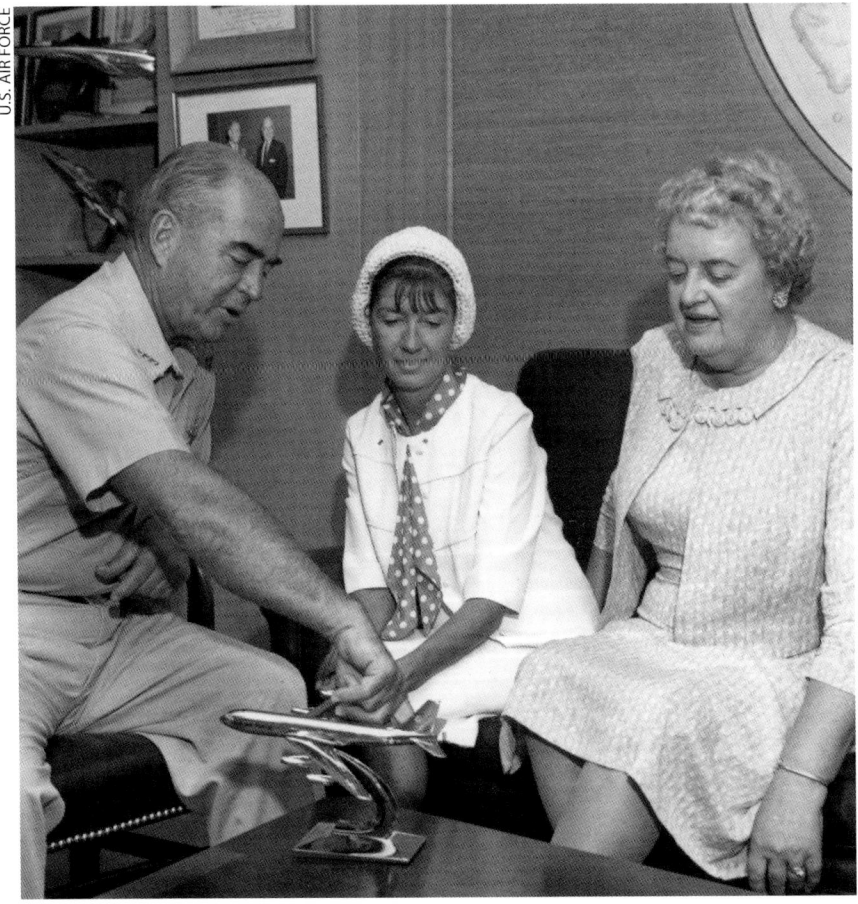

Opposite: A boy and his mom. When she came to stay with us in Hawaii, my mother, Bessie, charmed a number of celebrities, including Dean Martin.

Some days at the *Advertiser* (*above and opposite*) were livelier than others.

I joined J. Akuhead Pupule (*bottom, at right*) and friends in welcoming Hedwig von Trapp to the Hawaii premiere of *The Sound of Music*. *Below*: with Mr. and Mrs. Jack Soo (a.k.a Goro Suzuki) and Duke Kahanamoku. *Opposite*: With Arthur Godfrey at the KONA-TV studios

Frank meets my daughter, Kerry, as her proud daddy looks on. *Opposite*: Anything for a gag at the Don Ho & the Aliis show, a long-time Waikiki fixture at Duke Kahanamoku's in the International Market Place.

Fellow *Advertiser* columnist Bob Krauss (*lower left*) and I greet the King aboard the *Lurline*. *Opposite top*: Elvis and I share the microphone at the press conference preceding his "Aloha From Hawaii" satellite TV special in 1973. *Opposite bottom*: Col. Tom Parker and I sell programs during intermission at Elvis' Arizona Memorial benefit concert at Pearl Harbor's Bloch Arena in 1961.

A double date with Max and Helen Winter; Max owned the Minnesota Vikings. *Bottom*: Comparing notes with animal trainer Clyde Beatty (*center*) and boxing great Jack Dempsey.

to really throw a right hand correctly." Donald continued his drinking, and I'm sure totally forgot the discussion.

The next night, I had my "fight expert" hidden behind the house. Again, we started to discuss boxing and how to throw the right hand properly. I finally yelled out for my expert to please present himself.

Out marched Rocky Marciano, the famous heavyweight champion of the world who retired with an unbeaten record. Donald almost fell over! He was a huge Rocky fan. Rocky was his idol. My surprise worked.

How did I pull it off? I had received a call from Rocky's manager, Fred Petty, who asked if I would check in with Rocky and offer some aloha while he was in town. Petty was an old friend from Boston. I had invited Rocky to see Donald's concert, told him what a great fan he was and worked out the surprise appearance.

We had a film projector set up, and Rocky brought many of his most famous fights. He personally narrated the events.

For those who may not know, Rocky had forty-nine fights and never lost. But he came close on September 23, 1952, when he fought the champion, Jersey Joe Walcott. Some have called it one of the greatest punches of all time. Rocky was losing the fight. Then, in the thirteenth round, Rocky threw a perfect right hand that landed flush. Falling in slow motion, Jersey Joe slumped to the canvas. It took several minutes to revive him.

The *Rocky* movies were said to have been inspired by Marciano's career.

A day before his forty-sixth birthday, on August 31, 1969, Marciano was tragically killed in a private plane crash in Iowa. He was en route to a birthday party.

Fast Fact: Rocky Marciano

In the late 1960s, Rocky Marciano and Muhammad Ali actually "met" in the ring—to film a fight that was based on statistics fed into a computer. The "SuperFight" was shown in 1,500 theaters across the United States in January 1970. In the fantasy fight, Marciano KO'd Ali with a left hook in the thirteenth round.

NINE

Elvis Presley and Colonel Tom Parker

Toward the end of 1972, Matt Esposito, then manager of the Honolulu International Center (now the Neal Blaisdell Center) got on the horn. "I've got Col. Tom Parker here, in person, with a pretty good story," he told me.

"What a coincidence," I replied. "I wrote a letter to Parker yesterday, but my secretary forgot to mail it."

"Then come on over and deliver the letter in person," Matt said, laughing.

I hopped right over. I hadn't seen Parker since the benefit Elvis Presley did at Bloch Arena nearly a dozen years earlier, in 1961, at Pearl Harbor to raise money for the *Arizona* Memorial. Thanks to that concert, the *Arizona* project, after a lengthy financial struggle, was finally completed.

The story behind that story was this: the people in charge of fund-raising had asked *Advertiser* editor George Chaplin to help their cause. They were desperate. Ever the obliging sort, George wrote a special editorial asking for help, and he sent it to newspapers around the country.

That produced a long-distance phone call from Col. Parker. "I just read your piece about the *Arizona* Memorial problem," he told George. "What can my boy Elvis and I do to help?"

The Colonel and Elvis agreed to come to Hawaii and perform a special concert at Pearl Harbor. At the time, the Pacific War Memorial Commission had just a few thousand dollars in its bank account. Parker and Elvis not only raised $67,000 with the concert—big bucks in those days—they also spent about $25,000 of their own money in travel expenses.

Chaplin assigned me to assist Parker on the day of the concert. He also told me to cover the event for the paper. At intermission, Parker grabbed a large handful of programs and yelled, "Let's sell 'em!" As he plunged into the audience hawking the programs, he told me to take whatever money is offered, and added, "Don't give back change."

That was the start of our friendship.

Back to lunch with Col. Parker and Matt Esposito: the Colonel explained the purpose of his Honolulu visit. Elvis, he said, was going to do the first worldwide satellite TV concert from Honolulu. One billion people were expected to watch the event on TV!

When he finished, I made a pitch to Parker. I asked him if there was any way I could tie the event in with my charity, the Kui Lee Cancer Fund.

The charity came about by accident. I had been hospitalized because of Bell's Palsy, a nerve disorder. The whole right side of my face was paralyzed. Completely frozen. I couldn't move a muscle. At least my neurologist, Dr. Stanley Batkin, assured me I had not had a stroke, as I first feared.

Originally from New York, Batkin got through college by playing the sax. He and I hit it off instantly. At the time, Batkin also had a small laboratory at the University of Hawaii, where he was working on a cure for cancer. He told me he was down to his last few experimental mice and was desperate for funds.

That was the impetus to start the Kui Lee Cancer Fund, which was named for the great songwriter, Kui Lee, who died in 1966 of cancer at age thirty-four. In the beginning, *I* was the fund. Just me. Through my newspaper column, however, a few thousand dollars in change began to trickle in.

After telling the Colonel my story, he went into his act. Always the showman, he got up and began pacing, puffing away on his ever-present cigar. Parker explained that the worldwide Elvis show was basically going to be a television production, and there was seldom any charge to see a TV show in person. He was certain, however, that some kind of arrangement was possible. He asked me to come back the next day and meet with the RCA executives. Their permission, he said, would be the deciding factor.

After that meeting, I got the green light. It was agreed that those wanting to attend the concert could do so by donation only. It didn't matter if it was ten dollars or ten cents (and believe me, quite a few were admitted for only a dime). The first two major "donations" (tickets sold) were from Elvis and Parker themselves. Each contributed $1,000. The third ticket went to actor Jack Lord, who also donated $1,000.

According to the deal I made with the Colonel, I was to get the entire live gate of the television spectacular for the fund. In return, the *Advertiser* had to really get behind the concert and give Elvis a ton of publicity.

That was the Colonel. Always making a deal for his boy.

Naturally, the *Advertiser* went all out. After the concert, I received a check made out to The Kui Lee Cancer Fund for more than $75,000. That was big money in those times! Elvis and Parker even took out full-page ads in the paper, thanking one and all for attending the show and for making their donation to the cancer fund.

Incidentally, not a single cent of the fund was ever used for salaries, or expenses of any kind. Every penny went to charity—up until the time I had to turn the funds over. Because the fund was now quite substantial, Chaplin "suggested" I turn the funds over to a legitimate organization for administration. I argued that this could possibly dilute the funds I had earmarked for the University of Hawaii and for Dr. Batkin's cancer experiments. But Chaplin was very persuasive. I gave the entire $250,000 fund to the American Cancer Society. The University and Dr. Batkin, in return, received only a pittance from the money I raised over many, many months.

Elvis and Parker, the superstar and the manager, were like night and day. While Colonel was the ultimate talker, Elvis Aaron Presley was extremely shy. I remember the first time I met him in 1956. I, along with several other journalists, got to interview him on the *Lurline* as it sailed into Honolulu Harbor.

My first impression of Elvis? He was absolutely devastating to look at. He had perfect features, an unblemished complexion and slick, jet black hair. He was dressed casually, but still made quite an impression on us.

Because the hype about him at the time was so heavy, I was expecting Elvis to have a more aggressive attitude, armed with fast quips and personality galore. Instead, as I said, he was very shy. Just a kid, really. Interviewing him was almost painful, like trying to squeeze juice out of a frozen orange. Most of his answers were "Yes, sir" or "No, sir."

At first, I thought it was an act. How could someone so dynamic and expressive on stage be so non-communicative in private? I soon realized, however, that Elvis was simply being himself. At the time, I doubt he had any idea why fans reacted to him the way they did.

Now, Col. Parker, he was another story.

Parker loved talking about his early days as a struggling carnival con man. "I was always broke but always went first class," he said, relating one of his favorite stories. "Once, I checked into a fleabag hotel and asked for the best suite. It went for $12 a day and had cobwebs on the ceiling. I called the hotel manager to my room. 'This is the finest hotel I've ever seen, sir,' I told him. He was so shocked, he insisted I be his guest for the rest of the week. Nobody had ever complimented his hotel before!"

Parker smiled and added, "That will give you an idea of my snowman ability." To Parker, a "snow job" meant "hoomalimali," or plain old B.S.

"Another time, with not a penny in my pocket, I walked into a restaurant in a small Southern city and ordered their best steak," he told me. "Then I insisted on meeting the chef. "Your food is great, sir. You must be the world's best chef. May I have the check?" Of course there was no check for the rest of the time I was in that town with the carnival. A little snow job always did the trick."

Another of Parker's favorite stories about his carnival days involved his "dancing chickens." Always trying to hustle a buck, Parker came up with a new gimmick for an act. He got a gas hot plate and put a little curtain around it. This was his "stage." He barked, "Come see the dancing chickens." When a crowd gathered, he brought out a couple chickens, put them on the plate and turned on the gas to make the plate hot. That's how the chickens "danced."

Parker could never resist being a "snowman." (Not to be confused with showman!) Once, a public relations executive called him from London, claiming that he was one of the finest PR people in all of Europe and would love to handle Elvis.

"Why, that's just great," the Colonel said. "If you're that good, you can have the job. How does $50,000 sound?"

The guy was flabbergasted. He said, "That's just fine. I accept."

Then Colonel Parker nailed him with the punch line: "You have a deal—just as soon as *your* check arrives for $50,000." *Click.*

How much the Colonel really cared for Elvis, I don't really know. Honestly, I don't think there was a real personal connection. Elvis, I believe, both respected and feared him. Parker, however, was wily enough to know what he had, and he put his lifetime of experience into promoting this once-in-a-lifetime gold mine.

In all the years he and Elvis were associated, they hardly ever dined together. Parker explained it to me this way: "Elvis does the acting and singing, and I handle the business. We seldom see each other. He doesn't tell me how to do the business, and I don't tell him about entertaining or interfere in his private life. I'm often asked to manage other stars for large amounts of money. I tell them that Elvis is a full time job."

Elvis hung with his group, and Parker let him be. Elvis, in a way, was like Parker's trained seal. Parker told him what to do, and Elvis did it. Elvis got what he wanted, and so did the Colonel. It worked.

I have no doubt about one thing, however: Elvis loved Hawaii. He made some of his most successful films here and, of course, helped raise a fortune for local charities. He helped shine a spotlight on Hawaii and gave the state a king's ransom in publicity. The Colonel once told me that Elvis would have loved to have had a home in the Islands.

Few people knew Elvis as intimately as the legendary entertainer Wayne Newton. The two men had many things in common, including a love and passion for Hawaii. (Newton's first wife, Elaine Okamura, was from Hawaii, and he visited and performed in the Islands many times.) In his book, *Once Before I Go*, Newton wrote: "Deep down inside, Elvis was a lonely man who felt betrayed and abandoned. He found himself going from his dressing room to the showroom, coming alive onstage, only to return to the isolation of his hotel room. When you're that isolated, it can be hell. Elvis began to suffer the Howard Hughes syndrome. He became a prisoner of his own people."

When Elvis died on August 16, 1977, I had a hard time believing it. He was still so young. I knew he was deteriorating, but not to that extent. I guess only a few people knew how badly off he was.
In the end, as Wayne Newton mentioned in his book, I think he felt very alone. Most people figured he had the whole world in his hands. But to Elvis, he probably felt there was nothing left to live for. So sad.

Elvis had that indefinable something called, for lack of a better word, "stardust." Talent is one thing. Lots of people have talent. But when that certain gift is bestowed upon someone, and that gift is discovered, it weaves a magic spell over all who are exposed to it. Elvis had it in spades.

Like Sinatra and Brando and Muhammad Ali, he touched a chord in his audiences, and they reacted. There were better singers, and certainly better actors. But there was, is and always will be just one "King of Rock 'n' Roll."

That's Elvis.

Fast Fact: Elvis Presley

Worldwide, Elvis Presley has sold more than a billion records. He has 150 different albums and singles that have gone gold, platinum or multi-platinum in the U.S., far more than any other recording artist.

TEN

Frank Sinatra

This is about a Frank Sinatra few know. It deals with his "other" life—in Hawaii.

"Frank is coming in this afternoon on his way to Australia," *Honolulu Advertiser* managing editor Buck Buchwach mentioned one day in the late 1950s.

Now, with Buck, "Frank" could only mean only one person: Sinatra.

"Wanna meet him?"

He didn't have to ask twice.

Frank and Buck were longtime close friends. They'd begun their relationship a few years earlier, when Buck took a hiatus from the news biz to try his hand at public relations. Frank, was then at the lowest ebb of his career. Jobs for him were far and few between. His records weren't selling. His radio shows were canceled. He was dead at the box office. Nightclubs and television wouldn't give him the time of day. Frank's career was definitely on a downhill slide. MGM Studios canned him from its roster of leading men. Even his own talent agency, MCA, where he'd been a star for almost ten years, let him go. As hard as it is to imagine now, Frank was barely hanging on professionally. It looked like his time had come and gone.

Adding to his woes was his private life. It was a mess.

People were saying Frank was washed up. At that time, he was happy just to have landed a concert tour in Hawaii, playing—you won't believe this—a series of tent shows on sugar and pineapple plantations.

Buck was hired to handle Frank's public relations. And that started a long friendship between the two.

Buchwach loved to share stories of Frank's shows in Hawaii. Here was the one-time king of show biz, working in plantation camps for peanuts, but still performing as though he were headlining the most prestigious entertainment venues. He gave the people everything he had.

"I remember one time on Kauai, it was raining hard during his show," recalled Buck. "The audience was sitting on benches. Many in the crowd didn't know who he was. There was Frank, impeccably dressed in a tux, ignoring the rain dripping on his clothes while he sang his heart out. Never once uttering a complaint. I was never so impressed in my life. I became a fan forever."

"So, what's Sinatra really like?" I asked Buck on the drive to the airport to meet the legend.

"Depends on his mood." Buck replied. "If it's good, no problem. But if something irritates him or he's angry, get out of the way."

An example: in the mid-1950s, Frank abruptly cancelled his sold-out Australian concert tour. Seems a berth on the plane wasn't provided for Frank's accompanist. Frank flew into a rage, canceled Australia, turned around and went back to Hollywood. Even though the airline eventually straightened out the problem, it was too late. Months went by before Frank finally made up the Australian dates.

This time, Frank was stopping briefly in Honolulu on his way to another sold-out concert tour in Austrailia. At Honolulu Airport, a large throng of fans, dignitaries and local friends was on hand to meet him. Frank walked jauntily off his jet dressed like he had just stepped out of an expensive men's clothing store. Not a wrinkle in his attire! He was grinning from ear to ear. Charm oozed. He patted youngsters on the head after signing autographs. He shook all hands offered. It was an impressive performance.

Frank Sinatra first came to Hawaii in 1952 for two reasons: one, a honeymoon with Ava Gardner; and two, a concert at McKinley High School in Honolulu. Both events were successful. But it was an open secret that Frank and Ava fought like cats and dogs when they weren't making mad, passionate whoopee. However, Frank did find a new love during his visit—Hawaii—and returned to the Islands for one reason or another periodically over the years.

Of course, it was in Hawaii where Frank made the greatest comeback of his career.

Burt Lancaster once said, "It was obvious the instant he stepped on the set of *From Here to Eternity* and into the skin of scrappy Private Maggio, the role that would win Frank an Oscar—his fervor, his anger and his bitterness had something to do with the character of Maggio."

While Frank was putting out some of his greatest music in the 1950s and '60s, he was also cultivating a public persona that was close to self-parody. He was Frank the Swinger, the Chairman of the Board and Il Padrone to his "Rat Pack" pals Dean Martin, Sammy Davis, Jr., Joey Bishop and Peter Lawford. He called women "chicks," "broads," "dames" and "birds." He had affairs with almost anyone he wanted, and he had the pick of the crop. He reportedly slept with Marilyn Monroe, Kim Novak, Judy Garland and Lauren Bacall, and had flings and one-night stands galore. This was also the Frank Sinatra who allegedly kept company with some of the most notorious gangsters around: Lucky Luciano and Meyer Lansky, to name just a couple.

I remember attending the opening of Betty Reilly's nightclub in Waikiki in the late 1950s. Frank was hosting a small party of Honolulu friends. I was late because of deadline problems at the paper. When I arrived, the only chair open was next to Frank. So he motioned me to sit there. As host, he couldn't have been more charming. Made sure everyone had the best of everything the club had.

The next day at the *Advertiser*, I asked Buck about that tough-looking guy who was leaning up against the wall, watching our table all night long. "Oh," said Buck, "that was Sam Giancana, Mr. Chicago." At the time Giancana was one of America's most famous gangsters.

Frank's near-drowning in 1964 on Kauai made headlines around the world. He was in Hawaii directing and starring in a war movie, *None But the Brave*. Swimming one afternoon near the famed Coco Palms, where Elvis had recently made *Blue Hawaii*, Frank was caught in an undertow and swept 200 yards offshore. Fortunately, burly actor Brad Dexter, who was also in the movie, was on the beach at the time. He saw the star floundering and swam to his rescue. Because of the rough sea conditions and the undertow, however, Brad couldn't pull him in. All he could do was hold onto Frank until help arrived.

Lieutenant George Keawe of the Kauai Fire Department, who aided in the rescue, was quoted as saying, "In another five minutes, he would have been gone."

Frank later told the *Advertiser,* "I'm about the luckiest man in the world. Another few minutes out there and I would have had it."

Brad Dexter, at this point in his career, had made about twenty-five films and was an actor always in top physical condition because of frequent gym workouts. He had just come out of the water himself. "By the time I reached him," he said, "Frank had almost given up mentally and physically. His lips were blue and his eyes were almost closed. Frank just had no more fight left. I'm sure if I hadn't gotten to him when I did, they would have pulled out a dead man."

Then Dexter laughed. "You know something?" he said. "After Frank was rescued, I was left in the water. Everybody vanished. I didn't realize how exhausted I was. It was all I could do to make it back to shore. I'll never forget the experience as long as I live."

Because Frank was making his directorial debut in *None But the Brave,* his close friend Howard Koch, a top-notch producer-director, former head of production at Paramount and president of Sinatra's company, was on hand to help.

Howard and I were old friends by now, and he called to invite me over to see the production. I took a plane to Kauai one early morning and was met at Lihue Airport by Harry Friedman, a press agent for Warner Brothers.

We drove to the Coco Palms for breakfast and then headed to the set, seventeen miles away. On the way, Harry filled me in a little about the production. He explained that the movie was actually a co-production between Artanis Productions (that's "Sinatra" spelled backwards) and Tokyo Eiga Co. Warner Brothers was financing and producing the project.

Eventually, we turned off the main highway and bounced along a twisting dirt road, finally arriving at a small clearing. From there, we continued in a jeep to Pilaa Beach, miles from homes, stores or any sign of life except for a bustling motion picture company.

Frank was wearing shorts, a baseball cap with the movie's logo across the hat and a whistle hanging from his neck. As he was getting ready to film a scene, I asked how he felt after the near-drowning.

"Still a little shaky, but okay," he said. "Dean Martin called me. 'Drink, Frank,' he told me. 'Drink, but don't swim.' I never want to see water again. Matter of fact, I hardly ever go near it, anyway. I don't even swim in Palm Springs. I may stand up in my pool at home, but only up to my ankles."

Before shooting the scene, Frank huddled with Howard, then blew his whistle and yelled "Action!" After the scene was finished, Howard asked me if I noticed the huddle he had with Frank.

"Frank has never directed a movie," he explained. "It's a pretty expensive project. As talented as Frank is, do you think a major studio would trust him to direct? I'm here for insurance. We discuss every scene beforehand. I tell him what to do, and he does it. After all, I'm head of his production company."

A quick story about how Howard Koch and I became friends: early on in my career as a columnist, I received a press release from Kauai. A Hollywood company was filming a low-budget B-movie titled *Jungle Heat*, starring Lex Barker, a former film Tarzan, and the king of the horror movies, Boris Karloff.

What got my attention—and my blood boiling—were a few lines in the press release stating that the villain of the piece was a "local Japanese spying for Japan pre-Pearl Harbor."

Well, it was a well-known fact that not one American of Japanese descent in Hawaii was ever convicted of or involved in espionage or sabotage for the Japanese government. I ran an item in my column the next day, suggesting that people on Kauai working on *Jungle Heat* walk off the film until the script was changed.

Howard, as the film's director, called me.

"People are refusing to work on my movie because of that item in your column," he said. I explained my reason for writing it.

Howard flew over to Honolulu, and we had lunch.

"How can I change the script?" he asked. I suggested making the villain a Japanese national who arrives on Kauai via submarine—*anything*, I said, as long as the character wasn't labeled a local Japanese. Well, Howard changed the script, and that was that. However, when he returned to Hollywood, he called a press conference. The *Daily Variety* quoted Koch as saying that Hawaii's press was "dictatorial."

I immediately called Howard and said, "Hi, Howard, this is Hawaii's dictator."

It was the start of a long friendship between us.

Years later, in 1964, while visiting the World's Fair in New York, I got a call from the owner of a hot new restaurant, Voison, in Manhattan. He said, "My name is Hy Uycatel. A friend of yours in Honolulu made reservations for you at my restaurant. So please be my guest while you are in town."

During dinner, Uycatel sat with me and talked about all the famous people, including royalty, who had dined at his establishment. However, he confessed that he felt he really wasn't a success.

"Why?" I asked.

Said the restaurateur, "Until Frank Sinatra dines here, I won't think I've really made it. I've tried everything I can think of to get him to come here. No luck. I've asked many influential people to help me reach Frank. Still no luck."

After dinner, on the way out of the eatery to go to the theater, I asked Uycatel if I could make a phone call to the West Coast. I got hold of Howard at Artanis Productions and related the story about Voison.

Koch said, "Put the guy on the phone." Howard informed Uycatel that he and Frank planned to be in New York soon on their way to Italy to make a film called *Von Ryan's Express*. He added, "If my friend Eddie Sherman wants us to visit your restaurant, this is my promise that we'll be there. You have my word."

Uycatel's jaw dropped. He turned to me. "Who the hell are you?" he asked.

I smiled. "Just a little ol' Hawaiian menehune," I said, laughing as I exited the restaurant.

One day in 1961, I received a call from Mervyn LeRoy, who was directing the movie *Devil at Four O'Clock*, starring Spencer Tracy and Frank Sinatra, on the island of Maui. LeRoy was a legend in the cinema world, having directed almost 200 major movies, including that great all-time classic, *Wizard of Oz*.

"I'm celebrating my sixtieth birthday tomorrow," said LeRoy. "Can you fly over and be my guest?"

He didn't have to ask twice.

"Oh, and I'd appreciate it you keep anything you see and hear at the affair strictly off the record, okay?" LeRoy asked.

I agreed. After finishing my column, I dashed to the airport and arrived on Maui just in time to catch a chartered bus with some of the invited cast members. The bus took us to the Kula Lodge, high on the slopes of Haleakala.

Bill Blowitz, who was handling public relations for the film, greeted me at the door.

I walked in. There, right in front of me, were Tracy and Katherine Hepburn. They were sitting by the fireplace, holding hands. Turning to Blowitz, I said, "I had no idea they were a couple."

Blowitz responded out of the side of his mouth (a cigar was on the other side), "You must be the only newspaperman who doesn't know that Hepburn and Tracy have been together for years. It's a well-known 'secret' in Hollywood and maybe the only romance the press hasn't reported because of their respect for those two."

After dinner, LeRoy introduced various guests who told their favorite Mervyn LeRoy stories, many of which good-naturedly needled the director. But for some reason, he didn't call on Tracy to speak. Finally, and unexpectedly, this aging legendary star walked to the microphone, wished LeRoy a happy sixtieth, and told a few anecdotes about him.

Then, looking at Frank Sinatra, Tracy said, "There are a few of us in Hollywood besides Mervyn, who now belong to this special sixties club, including me and Jimmy Stewart. And Frank, you may not *look* sixty, but pal, you gotta *be* sixty" (which he wasn't at that time). That line drew a big laugh.

An attractive, white-haired aging couple, Mr. and Mrs. James, owned the Kula lodge. They watched the festivities from their office while holding hands. Never before did they have such a famous gathering of celebrities in their establishment. They were totally awed by the event.

I had learned that the Jameses had their entire life savings in the lodge and were on the verge of losing the place due to poor business. I told the story to LeRoy and asked if he would release me from my promise not to write about the party. I said that if I could write about it, the publicity might help their establishment.

Mervyn, however, was adamant. "You promised!" he reminded me. Then, after a pause, he added, "However, if you can clear it with Frank, then it'll be okay with me."

So we both approached Frank. He listened, then told LeRoy, "Look, Mervyn, Sherman's editor, Buck Buchwach, is one of my closest friends in Hawaii. I can promise you the story will come out just fine. So it's okay by me."

A year after the story ran in my column, I returned to the Kula Lodge. Mr. and Mrs. James were still in business. They told me: "After the story appeared in your column about all those famous people being here, we got all kinds of inquiries from the visitor industry. Reservations just poured in, and our business turned around."

On another visit to Hawaii in 1963, Frank hosted the Peter Lawfords, Dr. and Mrs. Leon Krohn, and few other friends for a week in Waikiki.

It wasn't one of Frank's happier Hawaiian stays, however. Lonely and still longing for his former wife, Ava Gardner, he flew in a different female companion every day from the Mainland. However, there apparently was a flare-up and Frank lost his temper. He took it out on the Moana Surfrider's hotel suite and smashed everything. He left the place in a shambles. He later apologized and paid the hotel for all the damage.

It's no secret if that if you were a friend of Frank's, he was loyal to you to the highest degree. In 1974, when he heard that Buck had a heart attack while visiting Europe, Frank quickly went into action. By the time Buchwach reached New York, arrangements had been to fly him directly to Houston, Texas, in Frank's private plane. There, the legendary heart surgeon, Michael DeBakey, was waiting.

DeBakey's appointment book was usually filled many months in advance. But when Frank Sinatra asked a favor, he usually got it. The operation was a success.

And, of course, Frank took care of all the expenses.

When Frank passed away in May 1998 at age eighty-two, the world lost one of its greatest entertainers, a man who had special meaning to anyone who ever heard his music or watched him perform—in person, on TV or in the movies. Oh, like everyone else, I've heard all the negative stories, but I only knew him as a kind and considerate man. He gave the world great happiness and joy. Not many people can say that.

Fast Fact: Frank Sinatra

Frank Sinatra was buried in Desert Memorial Park in Cathedral City, California, a few miles away from Palm Springs. Engraved on his tombstone are the words, "The Best Is Yet to Come."

ELEVEN

Henry J. Kaiser

The year was 1968. Walking through the Kaiser Hawaiian Village (now the Hilton Hawaiian Village Beach Resort and Spa) with my mother one day, I ran into the great builder, Henry J. Kaiser. He was in his eighties then.

Hefty, pot-bellied and bald, standing over six feet, he was still a physically imposing figure. We saw Kaiser's limo drive up, and it stopped right in front of us. He got out, and we enjoyed a brief chat.

After Kaiser was chauffeured away in his fancy car, my mother asked, "That man. He makes a living?" My mother had no idea who he was. When I later told him what she had said, he cracked up.

I spent many an evening at Kaiser's palatial estate in East Honolulu. There was no residence in Hawaii then that matched it. It was huge, sprawling and luxurious. It was located right on the water, out Portlock way.

He and his wife, Ali, loved poodles; they raised and showed them. The poodles lived in the lap of luxury. Special music was piped into their classy kennels. They had the finest food, veterinarians and caretakers. They even had their own secretary!

Mr. Kaiser, as most called him, was often alone at his plush, multimillion-dollar estate. He frequently called and asked me to bring any interesting visiting celebrities to his home.

I didn't want to impose on Kaiser, but I did invite a few luminaries to his lavish home. One was Burgess Meredith. The great film and stage veteran was anxious to meet this remarkable man. This was in the early 1960s, and Kaiser was one of the biggest television sponsors in the country. One of the TV shows sponsored by Kaiser at the time was the big hit, *Maverick*, starring James Garner.

Kaiser lectured Meredith on what he perceived to be the future of television. Basically, he said, "You ain't seen nothing yet." And he was right.

I remember the day Kaiser took me for a spin around a rural area of pig farms that would one day become the huge development called Hawaii Kai. Sitting in his pink (his favorite color) Jeep near Hanauma Bay, overlooking hundreds of empty acres below, he said, "Someday I'm going to build one of the most beautiful residential areas in Hawaii right down there. We will have thousands of homes. We'll have lakes and all sorts of things. You'll see."

I admit, I thought it was just his old age talking. Here was a legendary giant still reliving his many past successes, from shipbuilding and dam building to founding more than a hundred companies: Kaiser Aluminum, a chemical corporation, Kaiser Steel, Kaiser Cement and, of course, Kaiser Permanente, the giant health care firm.

Kaiser's health care plan was the first health maintenance organization (HMO) in the country and was later used as a model for federal programs. He even had high schools named after him that he built. And don't forget Kaiser cars.

All this was accomplished by a man who'd hardly had any schooling. Because he was so poor, he was forced to go to work at thirteen to help support his family. He had no formal education after that.

His shipbuilding statistics are staggering. During World War II, his shipyards built about 1,500 ships, sometimes completing a ship a week.

I've heard several different stories about how Kaiser came to build his Hawaiian Village. I prefer to believe this version, which was told to me by actor Bob Cummings. Bob was a frequent visitor to Hawaii, and among the reasons for his many visits was a lovely Island maiden he was absolutely stuck on. She happened to be a good friend of mine at the time, and she kept me posted—off the record, of course—on their romance.

In 1954, according to Bob, Kaiser and the top brass from his Oakland headquarters were huddled around a table loaded with blueprints in a meeting room of the Royal Hawaiian Hotel.

At six o'clock, a hotel employee entered the room and informed Kaiser and his men that they would have to leave the premises immediately because neckties were a "must" after six, and none of the executives, including Kaiser himself, were wearing any.

Naturally, Kaiser was infuriated. He vowed then and there to build a hotel in Honolulu where guests were not bound by any specific attire, where they could dress as they liked at any time, day or night.

Enter the Kaiser Hawaiian Village.

Because the Kaisers owned large show poodles, and because my wife and I at the time had a few tiny toy poodles of our own, HJK and I had common bond. I was then living in Windward Oahu right on Kaneohe Bay, which was very rural in those days. We had a pier and a speedboat and the house was on about an acre or so, surrounded by tropical foliage.

One day in 1968, our tiny toy Gigi was close to giving birth. She was so tiny—she weighed only about a pound and a half—and I was worried.

It was a Sunday, so there wasn't a veterinarian available. I decided to call Kaiser, the great industrialist, and told him of my concerns. I also invited him to a party we were planning that afternoon. Almost every Sunday, it was open house for visiting celebrities and friends. This helped me get a lot of items for my column. We would roll a long United Airlines red carpet from the top of our driveway down the hill to our house!

While gazing at the Kaneohe Harbor from my living room that morning, I suddenly saw two pink speedboats heading for my pier. I grabbed my binoculars. There he was, Henry J. Kaiser, the man himself, like he had nothing better to do, coming to the rescue of my little pregnant Gigi. Not only did he have his vet with him, he also brought a trainer, various assistants and a ton of food.

The vet took Gigi to Kaiser's personal dog hospital. Then we had a huge luau at the house that went on all afternoon.

Among the guests: famed pianist Victor Borge, the legendary Mills Brothers, the DeCastro Sisters and actor Rory Calhoun, who enjoyed cooking baked beans in a huge pot. That was some array of talent. The food, the company and the conversation were unforgettable!

After gorging ourselves, I invited everyone to play softball and badminton on our "private sandbar" located in the middle of Kaneohe Bay. The "island" became available only when the tide was low. And on this particular Sunday, it was perfect.

To get there, I transported them in my motorboat. I had to make a number of trips, back and forth, just a few hundred yards from my pier. It was a typical bright sunny day when the fun started.

As the afternoon wore on, however, storm clouds gathered. Then came the rain. It was pelting down! I was busy shuttling the guests back and forth as fast as I could, but they were all drenched. Back at the house, after toweling off, getting into warm clothes and imbibing a few brews, the gang of famous folks were mellow as they recounted the experience, all agreeing that it was the most fun they'd had in Hawaii, or anywhere else, in a long time. I often thought that if these special guests had performed at the party, it would have been one the greatest concerts of our time.

Oh, and Gigi? She gave birth at the Kaiser Kennels to a tiny puppy we affectionately named "Henry."

Of course, not all of Henry J. Kaiser's Hawaii ventures hit the jackpot. Among the disappointments was his venture into radio. The Kaiser station was KHVH. Kaiser recruited the best broadcasting talent in Hawaii at that time. That included Hal Lewis ("J. Akuhead Pupule"), Tom Moffatt and Ron Jacobs, who were the best-known of the talents that were lured with big salaries and other incentives. But it wasn't long before there were dozens of ex-employees.

Local boy Jacobs, a young deejay who went on to a highly successful radio career in Los Angeles, helped organize the Kaiser Station Alumni Association. In 1958, the ex-employees of Kaiser radio held an alumni lunch at the Tahitian Lanai, next to the Hawaiian Village. Ron emceed and the great man himself was "hanged" in effigy because so many were eventually pink-slipped. I was there to cover the event for the *Advertiser*.

Dozens of association members (and honorary ones) gathered

and were having a great time roasting the man they once worked for. Suddenly, there was a collective gasp and then a big burst of applause. The man himself, Henry J. Kaiser, joined the party. He was flanked by his wife, singer Alfred Apaka (his star singing attraction at the Village), and his administrative assistant, Bob Elliot.

I was sitting alone at a table when they walked over.

"Anybody else sitting here?" asked Kaiser.

"Just you and your guests, Mr. Kaiser," I smiled.

After everyone was seated, he leaned over and asked, "How's it going?"

"Not so good," I honestly answered. "They are giving you a good razzing."

Jacobs, on the mike, quipped, "Well, folks, as you can see, the man responsible for this gathering has honored us with his presence. I wonder if he'd like to say a few words?"

Not only was it totally unexpected that Henry Kaiser would attend such a function, but to get up and speak to this group of ex-employees? It was surreal.

Kaiser took the microphone and told everyone that he understood how they all felt. It wasn't anything personal. It was just a financial decision on the part of his company executives back in Oakland. The radio station was a fianacial disaster.

Henry said he knew what it was like to be fired. He then told the story of how, as a young man, he worked for a company that he believed couldn't get along without him. Then one day, he was let go. "I was devastated," he said. He left, got another job and worked so hard he was eventually rehired by the company that fired him.

"So I have a deep kinship with people who have been fired," he said.

An unexpected round of applause followed. Then Jacobs presented Kaiser with a "gift" of Reynolds aluminum foil. Kaiser laughed and accepted it graciously. One of his companies, you see, manufactured Kaiser aluminum foil.

That started a parade to Kaiser's table by ex-employees who wanted to shake his hand and tell him what a great sport he was.

"What a sense of humor," they were saying; "the guy can really take it."

His parting gesture was to instruct the Tahitian Lanai staff to serve drinks and food, on him, to everyone for as long as the party continued.

Henry J. Kaiser had arrived to boos and hisses, and left to cheers and applause.

Fast Fact: Henry J. Kaiser

Henry J. Kaiser's grandson, Edgar F. Kaiser, is a former owner of the NFL's Denver Broncos.

TWELVE

JACK LORD AND *HAWAII FIVE-O*

In 1968, a young, successful movie and TV producer-writer named Leonard Freeman arrived in Honolulu with an idea for a series based in Hawaii. His mother-in-law, who lived in the Islands at the time, had suggested that he look into the possibilities of producing such a show.

Thus was born *Hawaii Five-O*—the long-running police drama starring Jack Lord as top cop Steve McGarrett.

It wasn't an easy birth. This was one of the rare times in the TV industry that a weekly series was considered for production away from Hollywood. The logistics were expensive and fraught with potential problems.

Little by little, however, the pieces came together. Determined to succeed, Freeman overcame most of the hurdles. Still, the show's first season proved to be very difficult, even though the series got a solid hold in its time slot and appeared to be a hit during the first few months it aired.

Then, out of the blue, Freeman was told *Five-O* was being moved to another night and time slot. He was crushed, and furious.

When he and I discussed this, I learned that the new night would be Christmas. He was really angry because the show was just getting a toehold in the ratings. It suddenly dawned on me, however, that this might be a blessing in disguise.

I told Lenny to pray for snow on Christmas Eve. If it snowed, I reasoned, people would be home. It would be the perfect time for a cold, shivering nation to view *Five-O* with Hawaii's beautiful, sunny Polynesian background.

Guess what? It snowed. And the show demolished its competition in that new time slot. *Five-O* became a tremendous hit, and it would continue to be a hit for the next twelve years.

The *Five-O* production people set up shop in an old warehouse near Pearl City, a quiet little town in central Oahu, about a twenty-minute drive from Waikiki. When it rained, the warehouse roof leaked, and rats often nibbled at the various electrical cables. Production problems mounted.

After the show had completed its first season of episodes, I had dinner with Lenny.

Lenny said "Well, Eddie, I've decided to take *Five-O* back to Hollywood. We'll do all our interiors there. We just can't work under our present conditions. We're getting no cooperation from the city or state. Adios, Paradise."

I pleaded with Lenny not to take the show back to the Mainland.

"I really have no choice," he replied, shaking his head. "Not unless some kind of miracle happens and I find the right facilities to do my interiors."

A week or so later, I had a meeting with Hiro Yamamoto about the possibility of building a sound stage for *Hawaii Five-O*. Hiro was a successful developer and owner of his own finance company. I explained the biggest problem that the show faced: no sound stage to do their interior scenes. Hiro seemed interested in helping.

"What happens if I build this sound stage and offices, and the show gets canceled?" he asked.

I said that since the stage is basically a warehouse, it could easily be moved to Sand Island, an area that has many such buildings for storage, warehousing and other commercial uses. In that case, he would not really lose anything. Hiro suggested another meeting, this time with his lawyer and partner, Sakae Takahashi, who was a World War II hero, state senator and successful lawyer and businessman. Together, Hiro and Sakae took the idea to their friend, Governor Jack Burns. Burns agreed to cooperate wholeheartedly and gave them the green light to proceed.

A large parcel of land was selected on the slopes of Diamond Head, and then construction began. The project took thirty days.

I was on the site daily, filming the construction of the future *Five-O* soundstage with my Super-8 camera. Others also came to watch, wondering what was happening.

Jack Lord dropped by occasionally, making faces for my camera. He liked to stick his tongue out at me.

After the project was completed, Hiro, Sakae and I had another meeting to determine who would be president.

I said, "Hiro, of course." After all, he built the studio.

"No," Hiro shook his head. "I can't. I'm just too busy for this sort of thing."

"Then you, Sakae," I said

Again I was rebuffed. "Sorry, Eddie. I have the law practice, the Legislature and my business. It's impossible," said Sakae. "Hiro and I feel you'll do fine as president. You write about these people, and you have a lot in common with them. You understand show business. Congratulations. You're the president." And that's how I came to hold that position for nearly four years, until the facility was eventually sold to CBS.

When I told Lenny Freeman that he had a brand-new studio, he couldn't believe it. He was thrilled beyond words!

One night, Hiro, Sakae, Lenny and I were enjoying a nice dinner. Hiro said that he'd like to give Lenny some stock in the studio in appreciation of *Five-O* being a tenant in his new facility. Lenny explained that he couldn't take the stock from Hiro, that it would a conflict of interest. Besides, he said, he was already well compensated by CBS as the creator, writer and producer of the show.

Hiro said that he would place the stock he offered to Lenny in his office files. It would be available any time, he assured Lenny, should he ever change his mind.

Fade out, fade in: a few years passed. *Hawaii Five-O* had become one of the CBS network's most solid and reliable hits.

I was with Paul King one night in his room at the Kahala Hilton while he was packing for his flight to L.A. King was the CBS executive attached to the show. He was also a writer and producer for the network.

Turning to me, Paul said very seriously, "Sorry to tell you this, Eddie, but your friend Lenny is in big trouble."

"What's the problem?" I asked.

King said that he was tipped off that Lenny Freeman had stock in the Hawaii studio, and that, without question, it was a conflict of interest. The facts would be reported to CBS, and Freeman would have to be dealt with by the network.

I asked how King found out. At first, he was reluctant to tell me. Finally, after much prodding, he relented and informed me that someone told Jack Lord that he had seen a file in Hiro Yamamoto's company office that contained Freeman's stock in the studio. Lord, in turn, informed CBS.

I raced home, called Lenny in Beverly Hills and related the story.

Calmly, Freeman asked me to do the following: get a letter from Hiro and pre-date it to the time the studio was built. In the letter, Lenny wanted Hiro to explain about the shares that he offered—tell the facts as they actually happened, including explaining that the stock certificates would be in his files any time Lenny wanted them.

Hiro did just that, and I mailed the letter to Lenny. When the CBS bosses eventually called Lenny for an important meeting a few weeks later, he brought along his briefcase with that letter.

Sure enough, the CBS suits brought up the matter of the stock certificates. They told Lenny that he could be charged with improper conduct and so forth. At the right moment, Lenny whipped out the letter and explained what happened. The red-faced brass quickly offered their apologies.

Then, Lenny told the executives they had better read their contract with him. *Hawaii Five-O*, he said, was introduced on the TV screen before every episode as a "Leonard Freeman Production in association with CBS."

That, in effect, meant that Lenny had control of the show, including who could be hired—and fired.

Lenny informed the CBS brass that he would be getting on a

plane to Hawaii right away, and the first order of business upon landing would be to visit Jack Lord and fire him.

"I don't need the star of my show stabbing me in the back," Lenny said.

After he arrived, Lenny and I had breakfast at the Kahala Hilton. "Now, wait here," he told me. "I'm going next door to Jack's apartment and fire that son of a bitch. When I come back in a few minutes, you can announce that the new top cop on the series will be Lloyd Bridges."

I waited.

And waited.

Finally, Lenny returned.

"Well?" I asked.

He sat down, sighed and said, "Have you ever seen a grown man cry?"

After Lenny confronted Jack, the *Five-O* star nearly became hysterical. He said he did what he did because he thought it was in the best interest of the show. He said he didn't mean to get Freeman in trouble. According to Lenny, Jack then prostrated himself on the floor, grabbed Lenny around the ankles, begged for forgiveness and sobbed.

"I just couldn't fire him," Lenny said, "On the positive side, he's a hard worker. He's dedicated to the show and does a first-class job. But I told him to just stick to his work and mind his own business—that one more stunt like this would be cause for dismissal."

With that crisis averted, *Five-O* continued its roaring success. And my friendship with Lenny Freeman continued strong.

With *Hawaii Five-O*, Lenny proved to the network that he could produce a successful series on location far from Hollywood. In fact, Lenny planned to base his next TV series in Singapore.

Shortly before that announcement was made, I accompanied Lenny to Asia to scout locations. Day after day, we were chauffeured all over Singapore—a throbbing, exciting city-state with very strict laws. One day, unthinkingly I threw a cigarette on the street—I still smoked in those days—and was cautioned never to do that again. It could possibly mean jail time and a fine.

On this trip, Lenny asked if I would be interested in joining his production company. Naturally, I was very flattered—and very interested. But I told Lenny that I had no experience.

"Don't worry about it. I can teach you," he assured me. "Besides, what you've already done for *Five-O* for free is a pretty darn good audition."

He offered to be my mentor in the writing and producing areas of television. I didn't have to think about his offer for very long. Me, an executive with Leonard Freeman Productions? I couldn't wait! It was a dream come true.

But first, said Lenny, he had some minor stomach surgery to take care of.

Lenny's real problem—a fact that he hid from everyone—was his ailing heart. A world-renowned surgeon operated on him.

Lenny died in surgery. He was only fifty-three. And my future career a writer-producer in Hollywood also died.

I have so many *Five-O* memories. One day in 1972, I got a call from Israeli show promoter Danny Ben Av, who was winding up a Honolulu vacation with a friend. That same day, I was planning to attend a little cocktail reception at the Kahala Hilton for Mike Douglas, who was then one of television's top daily talk show hosts. So I invited Danny.

"Can I bring my friend?" he asked.

"Who is it?" I said.

"Topol."

"Topol? The star of the *Fiddler on the Roof* movie?"

"Yes."

"Absolutely, you can invite him; you *better* invite him!" I yelled into the phone. I was a big fan of Topol.

When I met him, I was amazed to see that he didn't even close to resemble the movie character he portrayed. In the film, Topol played a fat, bearded, middle-aged dairy farmer. In person, Topol was a clean-shaven, thin young man with a charming personality.

Jack Lord was holding court when we walked in. "Who are your friends?" he asked. When I introduced Topol, Jack's smile turned into a snarl.

"What's the gag, Eddie?" he said.

"No joke, Jack. This is Topol," I replied.

"I don't believe you, Eddie. I saw *Fiddler*. There's no resemblance at all."

"Okay, ask him yourself," I suggested.

Topol seemed to be enjoying it all. He just stood there, smiling the whole time.

Jack looked at him and said, "If you're Topol, do you mind proving it?"

Most of the guests were crowding around by now.

Topol spread his arms out (just like in the movie) and began snapping his fingers and humming.

Then, in his distinctive baritone voice, he starting singing at the top of his lungs, "If I were a rich man…"

Jack wrapped him in a warm bear hug. "It *is* you," he grinned. "What an honor it is to meet you!"

The whole room burst into applause.

From the time *Five-O* began, Lenny was always asking my then-wife, Peggy, if she'd consider coming out of retirement to play Steve McGarrett's secretary in the series. She always refused. Among other things, she felt it was a little demeaning for her to play a bit TV role when, in her day, she and Donald O'Connor were film stars with their names prominently displayed on movie marquees.

I reminded Peggy that that was another time. I also told her that being in *Five-O* could be fun; also, it would get her out of the house, and she'd only have to work one day a week. Besides, it would be a special favor to Lenny.

It took a while, with lots of prodding from me, before Peggy finally said yes. The job lasted eight years. Her name in the show was Jenny. The character was named after Leonard Freeman's late mother.

One of McGarrett's police gang in *Five-O* was a big, burly

Hawaiian professionally known as Zulu, whose real name was Gilbert Kauhi. Zulu was a popular Hawaiian entertainer and nightclub comedian. He was always in demand. Audiences loved him, and he became one of *Five-O*'s favorite personalities.

The show gave him international exposure and fame. His career was skyrocketing. No doubt, Zulu had a big future.

Then, in 1973, he made a fatal mistake. While shooting a street scene in downtown Honolulu, Zulu spied the show's publicity man, Len Weisman. Len was a Hollywood veteran who once worked for the legendary Howard Hughes. On the *Five-O* set, Weisman answered only to Jack Lord.

Zulu walked over to Weisman between takes and began needling him about not getting enough publicity. Weisman explained that he only worked for Jack.

Zulu increased his vitriol at Weisman for not publicizing him more. The needling inexplicably turned into some vicious, anti-Semitic remarks.

Weisman was stunned at the attack. He didn't know what to say. Those who witnessed the verbal fireworks were also stunned. Nobody could figure out what caused it all. Weisman, verbally battered, retreated to his office.

When Jack Lord returned to *Five-O* headquarters after finishing his scenes, he saw Weisman with his head resting on his desk. Jack asked what was wrong.

"Oh, nothing. I just don't feel well," said Weisman.

That answer was not good enough. Jack knew better. He wanted to know what the problem was, and kept after Weisman to tell him. Finally, Weisman explained what had happened with Zulu.

Jack hit the roof. He immediately went to the phone, called Lenny Freeman in Los Angeles and said he would not return to the set until Zulu was off the show. Permanently.

Zulu quickly got the word. He was through. Fired.

A few days later, Zulu came to my office at the *Honolulu Advertiser*. He was heartbroken. Totally dejected.

"I really didn't mean anything," he told me. "I like Len. I just got mad at not getting more recognition on the show. That's all."

He asked for my help. He wanted to explain his side of the story.

I told Zulu it was too late. He had really committed show biz *harakiri*.

News of his anti-Semitic attack against Jack Lord's publicity man was all over Hollywood. Suddenly, Zulu's future engagements for various personal appearances were cancelled. Professionally, he was treated like he had a contagious disease. Doors slammed in his face. The poor man was devastated.

He never worked on another TV show again. Overnight, Zulu went from a thriving show business career to professional oblivion.

More behind-the-scenes tales from the *Five-O* series: Bernie Oseransky, head of production for the show during its entire twelve-year run, recalled the time Jack screamed at Bill Finnegan, who produced the show for many years. Jack told Finnegan to "Get off my island." Of course, Finnegan refused Jack's "order." So Jack boycotted the show for a week until Hawaii Governor George Ariyoshi intervened and talked him into returning to work.

Jack involved himself in every aspect of the show's production. He was a perfectionist and expected everyone to measure up to his exact standards. He also involved himself in many employees' personal matters. Once, while walking near the Diamond Head sound stage, he passed a carpenter working on the production set and said hello to him. The carpenter, obviously somewhere else in his mind, didn't return the greeting. Jack took this as a slight and had the man fired.

Basically, Jack was a loner. He seemed to trust only his wife, Marie. She was his everything. They were totally devoted to each other.

Jack Lord—born John Joseph Patrick Ryan—grew up in the Hell's Kitchen section of New York and was, perhaps, Hawaii's most famous export. Many people believed that there was an actual Hawaii Five-0 police unit because of Lord's solid characterization and the show's gritty realism.

On a trip to London in 1972, while checking into my flight, I was asked to provide more identification. On a whim, I pulled out my special Hawaii Five-O badge that Lenny Freeman had given me as a present. It looked very real and was well made. As the airline employee scrutinized the badge, I looked both ways and put a finger to my lips, indicating, "Silence, please."

"Yes, sir," replied the lady. "Welcome aboard."

When the production ceased after twelve years and almost three hundred one-hour dramas, Jack shut himself off from just about everyone except his wife. He seldom ventured from his plush Kahala apartment, purchased during the early days of the show for $163,000—thanks to a loan from CBS. Today, that apartment would sell for many millions of dollars.

In his last days, Jack would occasionally be seen walking along the beach near his home, or shopping at Kahala Mall's Star Market. My last conversation with Jack was while he sat behind the wheel of his twenty-year-old Cadillac parked outside the shopping center. His car was showing signs of rust. He favored Cadillacs because he once was a car salesman for the company in New York during his days as a struggling actor. Jack was waiting for Marie, who was doing a grocery run inside the market.

Jack kept asking me the same questions, over and over, interspersed with various statistics about *Five-O*. It was very sad and disturbing to see his obvious mental deterioration.

Not long after that, on January 21, 1998, Jack Lord died of congestive heart failure. He was seventy-seven.

FAST FACT: JACK LORD

Jack Lord was originally considered for the role of "Captain Kirk" in the TV series *Star Trek*. Series creator Gene Roddenberry rejected Lord's demands to co-produce and have a percentage in ownership. The role, of course, eventually went to William Shatner.

THIRTEEN

Jack Paar

Hawaii was in a mild frenzy back in February 1960. The reason? Jack Paar, one of TV's most intriguing and enigmatic personalities, and the host of the popular *Tonight Show*, was in town to tape some shows.

Today, sadly, Paar may be all but forgotten. But in his day, he definitely was Mr. Big. Paar was the Johnny Carson, Jay Leno and David Letterman of his day—all rolled into one. He also had a few special "ingredients" that the other late-night hosts didn't have—namely, a penchant for emotional outbursts and a boiling feud with the media.

Although he professed to dislike controversy, he carried on much-publicized feuds with celebrities such as Steve Allen and national columnists like Dorothy Kilgallen, Walter Winchell and Ed Sullivan. Once, because the network censored a joke from a previously taped show, he walked off his show the next night and didn't return for a month.

Yes, he was a very sensitive, temperamental guy, as Hawaii and the rest of the country were about to find out again.

Paar's national TV show was broadcast from the Kaiser (now Hilton) Hawaiian Village's Ale Ale Kai Room before an audience of about 400 people.

Here are some of Bob Krauss' quotes about the event from the *Honolulu Advertiser*.

"Jack Paar made television history. He is the first performer to be booed by a Hawaiian audience.

"It wasn't a boo, really. Just a groan at a stupid, tactless remark that set the pace for a show set and some sort of record for insulting the audience and Paar's hosts in general. What made it really amazing is that neither Paar nor one of his guests seemed to be aware of what they were doing."

Bob's observations were right on the mark. The show was a mess. It all started when announcer Hugh Downs started warming up the audience before the show. He was doing fine, until the point where he said, "The people back in the United States…"

That drew a laugh from the audience. They'd heard it before. (Even today, almost fifty years after statehood, we hear visitors telling us, "You know, back in the states…") Everyone knew that it was an unintentional mistake. Hawaii had become a state just a year earlier, in 1959.

After the show got underway, however, Paar also made some reference to "back in the United States." To his surprise, he received only a horselaugh. He said it again, and got the same response. During an intermission, Downs took Paar aside and pointed out that Hawaii is, indeed, a part of the U.S.

To his credit, Paar came forward and apologized to the audience.

Then he began introducing several Island beauty queens by racial descent. Unbelievably, when he introduced the haole girl, Paar called her "the American" of the group.

Wrote Bob Krauss: "For a while, it was like amateur hour on a second-rate talent show. Paar forgot to introduce about half of the girls. Worst of all, he referred to the Hawaiian Village Hotel, where Henry Kaiser has ripped out a wall and put up bleachers in his dining room for Paar, as the Royal Hawaiian.

"All the while of course, Paar was doggedly sticking his foot in his mouth with the studio audience. He couldn't have made a bigger mess of it if it had been planned. Maybe it was.

"Whether it was laziness or just sheer ignorance, Paar seemed to bring out every tired and corny Hawaiian cliché—from poi and luaus to muumuus—that we've been suffering through for years. At any minute, I half-expected to have a fellow with a lawn mower come racing across the stage after a hula girl in a grass skirt."

And still, Paar kept talking about "those people in the United States."

Bob opined, "What got under my skin was not the stupidity of his mistake, but the insult that it implied—that Paar had never even taken the trouble to find out about the state he was visiting. That he was out here to bless Hawaii with his presence and expected us to watch with open-mouthed amazement."

Oh, but the story doesn't end there. The climax came after artist Peggy Cass came out and pretty much insulted everything Hawaiian. Then, inexplicably, Cass went into a rant.

"What are you so sensitive about?" she asked the audience. "Aren't you proud of being American?"

Yes, she really said that.

The audience sat in stunned silence. Announcer Downs tried tactfully to stop her. "Peggy…"

But she wouldn't let up. "I'm proud of being an American!" she said smugly. "I think everybody should be."

There was even more silence after her tirade. Comic Buddy Hackett, trying to lighten the mood, noted, "You know, I think we're going to get beat up."

Finally, Paar realized what was happening. It was like a light bulb went off in his mind, and he suddenly understood what he was doing wrong. After that, he tried hard—almost painfully hard—to say "Mainland" instead of "United States."

He even quipped that the people in Hawaii reminded him of religious converts; the converts, he said, were better believers than the people who converted them.

More silence. Nobody booed this time. As Bob mentioned in his story, by this point, everyone was feeling just a little ill.

There was much more Krauss had to say in his column about the fiasco. And so did almost the entire Hawaii press corps. After my wife Patty read this chapter, she told me, "I remember that show. My whole family watched it. I recall my mother [Yoshie Hoshino] saying about Paar, 'What a stupid man!'"

Because I had also interviewed Paar and we apparently hit it off, he called me asking for help. "They're killing me here," Paar said. "I didn't mean to say those things. I just didn't realize it was so derogatory. Can you help me straighten things out?"

I suggested Paar be my guest on my weekly TV show to tell his side of the story. Paar quickly accepted. The situation was somewhat straightened out, but people were still smarting over the incident.

About a year later, Honolulu was hit by a newspaper strike. Ironically, at that time, while I was out of work, I got an unexpected call from Paar in New York. He needed some film footage of the Hansen's disease settlement at Kalaupapa. "Just show what things look like there now. But, please, no full-on faces of patients. Backs of heads, or side shots," he said. He also instructed me to hire a camera crew and then send the bill to him. I hired two technicians and with a bunch of equipment we winged off to Molokai for the day. Paar edited the film into the homemade movies of his world trip that he featured on the network.

A few weeks later, I got another call from Paar. "So, where the hell is your invoice? I paid everyone but you." Shortly thereafter, a check arrived from Jack Paar for $1,000 with a nice letter of appreciation.

Fast Fact: Jack Paar

In 1959, Jack Paar interviewed Cuban leader Fidel Castro, a landmark segment that brought the TV host much criticism.

FOURTEEN

Jack Soo

In the early 1960s, Gene Kelly arrived in Honolulu to scout Asian talent for a Rodgers and Hammerstein musical he was planning to direct on Broadway. During his stay, he granted me an interview.

Like almost anyone who ever saw a Gene Kelly movie, I was a huge fan of this multi-talented actor and musical star. My first surprise came the minute we entered his suite at the Surfrider Hotel. Kelly took off his cap, revealing a completely bald head. Was this the handsome, athletic Gene Kelly of Hollywood fame?

Absolutely. Except for the hair. Apparently his hair had thinned out when he quite young. Kelly wore a toupee in all his films. It certainly was a good one. I never suspected.

I asked Kelly what he was doing in Hawaii. Was he here on vacation?

No, he said. He was here on business. He told me about his search for local talent for his new musical.

As Kelly unveiled the synopsis of the show, I became very interested in one of the characters he described: the nightclub emcee. I asked whom he had in mind for that role. He said probably Benson Fong, who had appeared as one of the sons in the old Charlie Chan films.

I interrupted Kelly, saying, "I just happen to know the best possible performer who can play that nightclub emcee. You've just got to see him and audition him. He lives in San Francisco."

Kelly laughed. "So besides being a columnist, you're also an agent?"

I told Kelly about my friend, Goro Suzuki. He would be perfect for the part.

"Well, as a matter of fact, I plan to visit San Francisco," Kelly said. "Where can I find this Mr. Suzuki?"

"The Forbidden City nightclub," I answered.

Kelly promised me that he would check him out.

Months later, while visiting San Francisco, I met up with Goro and his wife, Jean. I saw his nightclub show and had dinner with them.

During our meal, Goro asked me what I thought of his performance. I couldn't lie.

"You were awful," I told him. "I can't believe it. I haven't see you in about ten years and you're still doing the same crappy material you did back in Boston."

He hadn't added one new piece of material in all those years. He just didn't seem interested in his career. It was like he had given up. Goro admitted he was disillusioned with his life and career. It was so sad to see him like this. I believed he was special. All he needed was the right break.

Then I asked Jean what else was new. She brightened and smiled, "Guess who was in to see the show? Gene Kelly. He would like to audition Goro for a new Broadway musical if he'll come to New York."

"So?" I asked Goro.

"Not interested," he shook his head. "Why waste my time?"

I argued with him. Goro said Broadway salaries were small for secondary performers. He said he could make more playing clubs. He threw out nothing but negativity.

I pointed out that if he had a part in a Broadway hit, he could easily "double," meaning he could always play a top nightclub doing the last show after the Broadway performance. A gig like that would be very rewarding, financially. And being in a New York hit would also bring all sorts of possibilities in TV, movies and so on. It could open the door to stardom.

I talked and talked. Goro just sat there, smoking and drinking, and showing absolutely no interest. My argument fell on deaf ears.

He was so down that he had lost faith in himself.

Before I left, Jean said she'd work on him. She agreed with everything I said. I wished him luck and aloha and returned to Hawaii.

Goro, reluctantly, did go to New York. He auditioned for Gene Kelly, Richard Rodgers and Oscar Hammerstein, and he landed the job in *Flower Drum Song* as the nightclub emcee. The show was a big hit. A year or so later, the lead actor, Larry Blyden, left the production and Goro replaced him. Almost overnight, he was the new star in theater. Goro toured the country. He got out of debt. For the first time ever, he tasted fame and fortune. His life turned completely around.

Eventually, Goro was signed to play detective Nick Yamana in the TV sitcom *Barney Miller*. That series, which premiered in January 1975, was a big success and ran for many years.

Goro also guest-starred on numerous other TV shows: *Police Woman, M.A.S.H., Ironside, The Odd Couple* and *Hawaii Five-O*, to name just a few. He appeared in many movies: *The Green Berets* with John Wayne, *Return from Witch Mountain, The Monk, Thoroughly Modern Millie* and *The Oscar*, among others.

Finally, Goro was on top of the world. Fame and fortune were his. His old life was history. The financial struggles were over.

Then, unexpectedly, tragedy struck.

Cancer of the throat.

Goro fought it valiantly, but lost the battle.

My wonderful friend, Goro Suzuki, better known to millions around the world as Jack Soo, was gone. He died on January 11, 1979, of esophageal cancer.

Fast Fact: Jack Soo

Jack Soo and his *Barney Miller* character, Nick Yamana, were so beloved that a special retrospective episode was aired, showing clips of Yamana's best moments, at the end of the show's 1979 season.

FIFTEEN

James Clavell

James Clavell stood over six feet tall and was solidly built, with broad shoulders, a strong Scottish chin, brown eyes and a ruddy complexion. He limped out of his cottage at the old Halekulani hotel with a huge grin on his face. The year was 1966. He was carrying a large, yellow-jacketed book with huge black printing. He held it up over his head with great pride. It read: *James Clavell's Tai-Pan*.

"Look," he joyously said. "My brand-new baby. I just received this in the mail. Isn't it beautiful?"

I was there to interview the famous author, screenwriter and film director, and to witness this historical event.

"Must be quite a feeling," I replied, not knowing what else to say.

"Like giving birth, my boy, but maybe not as much pain," he laughed. "Let's go have a drink."

We sat at the Halekulani Terrace, sipping and talking while taking in one of the greatest sights the world has to offer: a Hawaiian sunset.

"What's your book about?" I asked.

Clavell smiled. "Well, I guess you could call it a swashbuckling tale of a pirate merchant in the 1800s," he said. "And, of course, it's set in Asia. I've always had the feeling that because of my love of the Orient, somewhere deep in my background, or maybe in another life, I was Asian."

If you've never read this Clavell classic, *Tai Pan* is a sweeping fictional account of the founding of Hong Kong. Full of adventure, romance, suspense and betrayal, it skillfully tells the story of Dirk

Struan, a merchant overlord. A *tai pan*. Struan builds a huge, successful trading company called Noble House. Along his way up the ladder of success, he has to fend off pirates and bandits and other antagonists.

Then Clavell told me about his very first book, *King Rat*. That novel was basically about survival in Changi Prison in Singapore during World War II.

"*King Rat* happened sort of by accident," Clavell told me. "I was sidelined at the time from my regular job because of a Hollywood screenwriter's strike. In other words, I was unemployed. Memories of my World War II experiences began to haunt me. So I began to write a novel about my prison life. That writing process released many suppressed emotions. Everything just poured out of me. I hammered away at the typewriter and had my first draft of the book finished in twelve weeks."

I was fascinated by him. Here was a man who, as a member of England's Royal Artillery, was captured by the Japanese in the jungles of Malaysia. It seemed that his life was even more interesting than his novels.

"It was 1942, and I was sent to the Far East," he continued. "I got my bad leg after being wounded by machine gun fire. For several months I hid in a Malay village. But eventually I was captured and sent to the notorious Changi Prison near Singapore. The conditions were unimaginable!"

Clavell told me that only a few out of some 150,000 inmates survived the severe incarceration. "It was the worst horror anyone can go through in life, and I was there for three and a half years," he said. "How I lived through it, I'll never know. But Changi was my university. It gave me an incredible strength, a special awareness of life. Just surviving the experience is like living many borrowed lifetimes."

Clavell got out of the service in 1946 and momentarily considered a career in law or engineering. But then he met his future wife, April, an aspiring actress, and became fascinated with directing and writing films.

"Eventually, we emigrated to the United States," he explained, "and after a brief stint in television in New York, we moved to

Hollywood. As a challenge, I wrote a screenplay, *The Fly*, a science fiction story, and somehow was able to bluff my way into a screenwriting contract. I knew I had found my profession."

After his successes with *King Rat* and *Tai Pan*, more bestsellers followed: I'm sure you've heard of *Shogun*, but Clavell also penned *Noble House, Whirlwind, Gai-Jin* and others. Meanwhile, his screen career was also flourishing. He produced and directed a slew of hits: *Watusi, Five Gates to Hell, The Great Escape, 633 Squadron* and *The Satan Bug*. One of his biggest hits, *To Sir with Love*, with Sidney Poitier, was a jackpot for Clavell because his contract called for a percentage of the action. The film was made for less than $1 million and grossed about $15 million.

Clavell was also executive producer of two TV miniseries that dramatized his novels: *Shogun* and *Noble House*. In 1988, an estimated 130 million viewers tuned into the twelve-hour *Shogun* miniseries. Richard Chamberlain, who now calls Hawaii home, played the hero of *Shogun*.

Some years after first meeting Clavell in Honolulu, I was in London. I called him, and he was nice enough to invite me to his new estate about twenty minutes by train from London. It was a twenty-four-acre estate with a sixteenth century manor house in Surrey.

When I arrived, Clavell spread his arms and said, "Not bad for a bloke who was once a prisoner of war!"

Clavell and April were in the process of renovating the property. Of course, no matter what condition the slightly run-down estate was in, it was still an impressive sight.

"What is it like to be the owner of such a beautiful place?" I asked.

I'll never forget his response.

"I don't really own this," he said. He then pointed to a plaque mounted over a door. It read, "In Life We Are Merely the Caretakers."

How true those words are.

James Clavell died on September 7, 1994, of a stroke while battling cancer in Switzerland.

Fast Fact: James Clavell

Born in Sydney, Australia, James Clavell became a naturalized United States citizen in 1963.

SIXTEEN

John Ford

The first time I met John Ford on-board his yacht, the *Araner*, at Waikiki's Ala Wai Yacht Harbor in the early 1960s, he was bare-chested and wearing a colorful lava-lava. He was as pale as a piece of porcelain, and only a few wisps of hair remained on his scalp. On one side of his mouth was half of an unlit cigar. Tucked in the other corner of his mouth was a dangling handkerchief to catch any strands of drool. Over his right eye was a big black patch.

Ford purchased this two-masted, 106-foot yacht in 1934 and christened her the *Araner* after the Irish island where his mother was born. This was where he usually retreated to prepare his pictures and rest after he made them. In other words, he used it every chance he had.

The Fords had spent half their lives on the *Araner*, cruising winters in Baja and farther south in Mexico, and many years in Hawaii, where their children were enrolled at Punahou School. More and more over the years, *Araner* became his refuge.

The boat was a comfortable ketch with room for all. It had two fireplaces and bathrooms, red carpets, a four-poster marriage bed and a dressing room for his wife, Mary. Ford used the teak deckhouse as his special area, where he drank and played cards with pals such as John Wayne.

Seeing Ford like this up close for the first time, I couldn't believe he was the legendary, feared motion picture director who reportedly made leading men quiver like Jell-O. This was the man they said was the greatest, toughest director of Westerns in the history of the film industry?

But it was him, all right. In person. He had aged quite a bit since I'd first caught a glimpse of him some twenty years earlier. Then, he was up in the crow's nest as a Naval officer filming a scene on the *Lurline*, the ship that first brought me to Hawaii in 1942.

Ford couldn't have been more polite and courteous. He showed me around his vessel and introduced me to some crewmembers. An hour later, I departed. I had finally met and interviewed the great John Ford.

When I got back to the *Advertiser*, I pulled out my notebook. I was stunned. It was blank. I was so captivated by Ford that I hadn't written a word. Instead of me interviewing him, he became the reporter.

Fortunately, I was asked back to his ship a number of times, and also to his home in Los Angeles. Over time, I learned a great deal about this incredible character and extraordinary film master.

Here's an excerpt from a column I wrote in January 1964 about Ford:

Frankly, when I went aboard the yacht, Araner, *berthed at the Ala Wai Yacht Harbor, it was just to say hello to John Ford and his wife, Mary, and spend a few minutes in their delightful company. The few minutes turned out to be a couple of hours of stories, gags and fascinating conversation. And doing most of the talking was a man of whom it can truly be said that he is a legend in his own lifetime, whose name is indelibly inscribed in American motion picture history.*

The first time I interviewed Ford many years ago, also aboard the Araner, *I was nervous. Maybe it was his reputation. For it was whispered that he-men like John Wayne quivered when Ford shouted an order on the set. I expected a gruff-voiced man. Instead, he was soft spoken.*

After asking a few questions in my most polite manner, he suggested, "Why don't you put down that pencil and stop trying to make like the great American reporter?" Before I knew it, he was interviewing me. The honor made me gush like a mynah bird. When we said goodbye, I realized I didn't have an interview.

This time he staggered me with his memory, recalling things we talked about years ago, even repeating jokes I told him at that time. He knew things about my personal life and my newspaper work, and told me what a fine actress my late wife was as a youngster when he directed her in his award-winning classic Grapes of Wrath.

First thing Ford does when he arrives on his yacht in Honolulu is dive over the fantail for a swim. While splashing around, his wife Mary asked him what time it was.

"How should I know?" he yelled.

"Well," said Mary, "you're wearing your watch."

As Ford climbed up the side of the yacht, some tourists sailed by, laughing and pointing. He had accidentally dropped his trunks, which were much too big for him. The trunks actually belonged to his 6' 4" grandson.

John Ford, who has never shared the wild life of Hollywood, or for that matter been anxious to have his name in the paper, asked me to help him decipher a couple of cables he had received from national magazines requesting interviews. It was like trying to read Greek. One from Cosmopolitan threw Jack completely. It read: "Understand nick name skipper or admiral. Is gag? Answer soonest—imperative."

Ford sent the following collect: "In answer to your cable of January 16, 1964, ever since I was brought up in Peaks Island, Maine, very close to the water, at the age of 4. I built myself a raft to go sailing. Then I rebuilt a small dory. Finally, as the years went on, I managed to save enough money to buy a boat which I have kept in Honolulu for the last ten years. This is where I spend my time between motion pictures. On the set, while working I wear a yachting cap with a long visor to save my eyes from the light as much as possible. This, plus the fact that I am a retired Rear Admiral in the Navy is probably why some folks call me 'Admiral.' I hope this answers your questions—soonest. Mahalo and aloha nui a ka ko. J. Ford."

It was no secret that Ford battled intermittent losing bouts with liquor for many years. I witnessed such a scene once that would have made a TV special had it been filmed.

One evening, in the *Araner*'s dining room, he and the great Irish actor, Richard Harris, were having a drinking contest. They matched each other, drink for drink. And as the evening wore on, they began to challenge each other with poetry and bits of Shakespeare. It was a contest, and I was the only other person there, watching and listening to these two great Irishmen battling each other with this duel of words. I left when both men finally passed out.

John Ford arrived in Hollywood before World War I. From then until his death five decades later, he made over 150 films, including the 1939 classic, *The Grapes of Wrath*. I had learned a little bit about the making of *Wrath* from someone who appeared as one of the children in that Depression-era slice of Americana.

Peggy Ryan played one of the children in the movie and had a few very dramatic scenes. At the time the movie was made, Peggy had no idea who John Ford was. He was just another director who, as she recalled, didn't act like a director. He was always cordial with the children. More like an uncle.

"He told me I should concentrate on studying dramatic acting and thought I had ability in that area," Peggy recalled. "Unfortunately, I didn't follow his advice."

Ford first discovered Hawaii in 1931, when he sailed into Honolulu on the steamship *Wilhelmina* with his wife. At the time, Mary Ford was angry at John for some reason or another, and he was trying to make up with her. The wealthy Big Island landowner Francis Iʻi Brown invited the Fords to his seaside cattle ranch in Kona, where the Ford marriage began to mend.

However, Ford's drinking got out of hand, and he returned to the Royal Hawaiian Hotel and stayed in his room for two weeks, drunk most of the time. Mary had to take him to Queen's Hospital because he was suffering from alcoholic dehydration.

Producer-writer Marty Rackin and I were quite friendly during the 1960s. He visited Hawaii often. He knew Ford well and told me many tales about the director. They first met when Marty hired Ford to direct *The Horse Soldiers*, a Western authored by Marty and his producing partner, John Lee Mahin.

It turned out that Ford had a lifelong fascination with the Civil War. This was when big stars were not bound by lengthy studio contracts, so they could demand large salaries and fees for each film. John Wayne and Ford received their biggest paychecks ever for *The Horse Soldiers*, plus a piece of the profits.

"I had to give them the moon in order to get their commitments," said Marty. "The film helped put me on the map."

Working with Ford, recalled Marty, was no picnic. Still, he added, "He could see more out of that one good eye than two producers see out of four."

A couple of other films that Ford made in Hawaii were *Mister Roberts* and *Donovan's Reef*. *Mister Roberts* featured an all-star cast, including James Cagney, Henry Fonda, William Powell and Jack Lemmon. On-location shooting started in September of 1954 at Midway Island and the Kaneohe Marine Corps Air Station on Oahu. Ford sent the *Araner* to Honolulu and moored her at the Ala Wai Yacht Harbor. The ship became his hotel suite and office, as well as an impressive stage for dealing with the various big egos working on the picture.

Henry Fonda had played the star role of Roberts on Broadway and felt he knew more about his character than Ford did. This, of course, led to major problems and fireworks between the two. And to think it all began as a dream reunion between them—they had worked so well together in *Grapes of Wrath*.

Ford began drinking, starting with a little beer. It got worse daily. Eventually, Ford holed himself up on the *Araner* and drank himself into oblivion. While he intended his ship to be a showplace, it instead became his hiding place. He refused to eat or see anyone for days, while the entire cast and crew waited for him to sober up.

Ford never finished *Mister Roberts*. The company returned to Hollywood, where Ford suffered a ruptured gall bladder and was rushed to the hospital. Mervyn LeRoy finished directing the movie. Ford spent six weeks recuperating from the surgery. Jack Lemmon's portrayal of Ensign Pulver won him the Academy Award for "Best

Supporting Actor."

John Ford's last film made in Hawaii was *Donovan's Reef*. It was sort of a farewell to th*e Araner* and a way of life that Ford could no longer support. In 1954, the ship sailed to Honolulu through a storm to be a home for friends and family while shooting the movie.

Ford had his family with him on this last Pacific trip, along with John Wayne, Lee Marvin and their families. They all had a good time on this movie, which was full of barroom fights, forgotten wars, pagan and Christian rituals, and all kinds of mayhem. When they started the film, there was only a ten-page outline. Eventually a haphazard script was fashioned, and all had a summer of fun.

Fast Fact: John Ford

When the production finished and the shooting was over, the *Araner* was sold for a song. It became a tourist cruise boat named *Windjammer,* leased by Patrick Brent, a former Marine and successful businessman.

The Ford era had ended, but his films will live forever.

SEVENTEEN

Judy Garland

One day in 1961, I got a call from Lou Robin, a longtime friend who was then the biggest concert promoter in America. "I'm presenting Judy Garland at the Hollywood Bowl," Lou told me. "Will you be my guest?"

I never said "Yes" so fast!

Judy Garland, the darling of Hollywood and, frankly, the entire movie-going world, had had her personal and professional problems over the years. Now she was on the comeback trail. This concert would be her first appearance in Los Angeles in many years. The Bowl was sold out, and scalpers were having a field day selling tickets.

I sat in one of the boxes in the first few rows at the Bowl. Each box easily accommodates a half-dozen people. I looked around me. All the other boxes were filled with some of the most famous faces in the world—from actors to producers, directors to media moguls. It seemed all of Hollywood's elite were here to pay tribute to their darling Judy.

Backstage, Lou told me later, there was much discussion about the rain clouds gathering over the open-air Bowl. But Judy wasn't concerned. "Don't worry about it," she told Lou. "The more humidity in the air, the better it is for my voice!"

What most people don't know is that Judy Garland suffered from stage fright before a concert. "You thought you were going to have to push her out onto the stage," Lou said, "but when she heard that first downbeat of the first song, that's all she needed."

Here are a few words about the concert that Dick Williams wrote for the *Los Angeles Mirror*: "I've seen some extraordinary sights over the years in covering show business, but none of them were more striking and few as memorable as the Judy Garland concert.

"On a damp, drizzly night much more suited to frog hunting or roasting chestnuts than sitting outdoors listening to a singer, a huge audience of 20,000 filled the Bowl and stayed until the last bell-like tones of this singer's singer had died away. Then with a mighty football throng kind of roar, they tendered her a last, final accolade."

Mimi Clark wrote in the *Los Angeles Times*: "The impact of a personality on the public can be such that an audience will endure bad weather, pay any price for tickets, and overlook any musical technicalities. Such a personality is Judy Garland. She held her audience spellbound. Even the orchestra joined the audience in a long standing ovation."

This was my review of the show:

HOLLYWOOD—In this space age, Judy Garland took 20,000 screaming hysterical fanatics "somewhere over the rainbow" for a two-and-a-half-hour talent display that will go down in the annals of show business history as one of the most electrifying performances ever witnessed.

I was reminded of a time when Al Jolson entertained a capacity audience at the Boston Garden, and I thought I would never see another living performer manipulate a throng with the same magic assurance.

But Saturday night Garland not only lived up to every rave notice received since her comeback, but hit an emotional peak usually reserved for a returning war hero, a home run in a World Series or a presidential candidate being nominated.

The Hollywood Bowl had been sold out for weeks. Tickets were scalped for as high as $50 a pair. The weather was threatening. As Judy walked on the stage for her first song, a slight drizzle fell. Nobody left his seat. The overture and umbrellas went up at the same time.

Behind Judy Garland were forty-nine of the best studio musicians in Hollywood. In front of her, a glittering array of filmland royalty. I saw many familiar faces—Rock Hudson, John Wayne, Danny Kaye, Louella Parsons, Hedda Hopper, Jack Benny, Robert Preston. The list goes on and on. Sitting beside me was Stanley Kramer, the producer-director who recently completed Judgment at Nuremberg, which brings Judy Garland back to the screen in a highly dramatic role that may add an Oscar to her laurels next year.

It was at least two minutes before she could sing her first song. A standing ovation greeted her. The first half of the program left something to be desired. Her choice of tunes did not include familiar Garland melodies. They were more conducive to the intimacy of a nightclub than the vastness of the Hollywood Bowl.

The applause was generous for each song, but the wild shouting heard on Judy's Carnegie Hall album was missing. Before intermission, Judy launched into "San Francisco" and gave an indication of what to expect in the second half of the show.

The bomb hit the bowl after "Rock-A-Bye." Garland had opened up that big, powerful, rich throbbing voice with such emotion that thousands were brought out of their seats as if somebody had lit a fire underneath them. The same thing was repeated after every song thereafter: "Swanee," "Chicago," "Somewhere Over the Rainbow," etc. Rock Hudson, sitting a few seats away, took off his shoe and was pounding the stage yelling, "More, more!"

The applause, screaming and whistling lasted a full five minutes when it was thought she had finished her show. Judy told the people she had used up every song in her repertoire. They wouldn't stop the demonstration until she agreed to repeat "San Francisco."

And a demonstration it was. People from all sections of the Bowl had left their seats and were kneeling in the aisles. It was as if an evangelist called.

When the performance was over and Judy had left the stage for good, mobs of people were standing and staring at the stage, numb from the impact of a little girl with big brown eyes who had finished one of the greatest performances I have ever seen in my life.

Two years before, she was considered washed up in show business. But this particular Saturday night, there was no doubt there's still a lot of punch in Judy.

When I arrived at the nightclub for Judy's private party, I happened to pull up just as she was getting out of her limo. So I followed behind her as she went around the entire room shaking hands, kissing friends and accepting her well-deserved compliments.

The memory of that night is still with me. And, every once in a while, I play that special tape in my head. It seems as fresh as always.

Fast Fact: Judy Garland

Every year on June 22, the state of Minnesota celebrates Judy Garland Day in tribute to the hometown star. The festival is held in Garland's birthplace, Grand Rapids.

EIGHTEEN

Kui Lee and Hal Wallis

It was a hot Sunday morning in 1980 when the phone rang.

I was living in Las Vegas at the time.

"Hello, this is Hal Wallis," the voice said.

At first, I didn't believe it. *Somebody's trying to play a joke on me*, I thought. As he continued talking, however, I began to recognize Wallis' deep baritone voice from past interviews and conversations that we've had over the years in Hawaii.

"To what do I owe the honor?" I asked the famed film producer.

"I just finished reading your script of *Kui*, and I'd like to have you come to my Hollywood office and discuss an option for a movie," he said.

Wow.

For a long time, I just sat there and tried to sort out my emotions. I couldn't believe it. I felt like I had suddenly won the lottery.

Weeks before, I had sent out my last few scripts about Kui Lee to various people in the film industry. Wallis was one of them. Kui was the legendary poet-songwriter-entertainer who died of cancer at the age of thirty-four. He left behind a treasure trove of the most wonderful music, packing incredible adventures into his life during the short time he had on Earth.

I knew Kui well. I covered him frequently during his engagement as the star at Queen's Surf, one of Waikiki's top nightclub's during the 1950s and '60s. Kui performed on the first floor of the club. Upstairs, Sterling Mossman held court at the popular Barefoot Bar. Between the two attractions, the club was packed on a nightly basis.

It was 1953 when Kui, then a Polynesian fire knife dancer in his early twenties, checked into the YMCA in New York with one suitcase containing his knives and costumes. The suitcase was promptly stolen while he was taking a shower. Fortunately, he saw the two thieves leaving his room and gave chase. Wearing only a towel, he caught up with the punks in an alley, and they wound up splattered all over the sidewalk.

Kui auditioned at the Hawaiian Room of New York's Lexington Hotel, a highly coveted showcase for Island performers. He not only performed as a fire knife dancer, he also directed and choreographed the entire production. During those years, Kui cut quite a swath through New York. Whenever he could, he visited various jazz clubs and sold his songs to anyone in show biz who was interested. Bobby Darin reportedly bought some of Kui's songs for $25 each.

In time, Kui worked his way up to a $2,000 weekly salary, which was big money for that time.

A lingering case of homesickness, however, brought him back to Hawaii. He left his wife, Nani, in New York and returned home. His songs were sensations in the Islands. "I'll Remember You," in particular, reached unbelievable heights of popularity. In fact, it became a signature song for Don Ho and was recorded by a long list of artists.

Then, at the age of thirty-four, the incredible talent of Kui Lee was silenced. He died on December 3, 1966, with Nani at his side.

His wake was held five days later at Kawaiahao Church in downtown Honolulu. Ironically, the historic church was built by missionaries, whom Kui loved to poke fun at in his nightclub act.

Kui's funeral was held the next day. Eulogies were delivered by some of Hawaii's most prominent citizens, including Governor John A. Burns and Honolulu Mayor Neal S. Blaisdell. Said the Mayor, "Honolulu lost a gifted young man, a new voice in tune with the modern rhythm of our metropolitan city, a haunting voice which never will let us forget our Hawaiian point of view."

Afterward, the funeral procession headed to the sea, where Kui's coffin was placed on the double-hulled catamaran *Ale Ale Kai V*. Throngs of people lined Honolulu Harbor as the vessel sailed out to sea, joined by an honor guard of outrigger canoes, with tape recordings of Kui's songs playing as fitting background music. As the catamaran approached Waikiki, "I'll Remember You" began to play.

Finally, three miles out to sea, the catamaran's engine slowed and the vessel turned to face Waikiki. The music stopped. Under a moody, gray cloud that hid the sun, Kawaiahao's Reverend Abraham Akaka sprinkled blossoms on the ocean's surface, reciting Bible verses in both Hawaiian and English. A flare gun went off, and a small plane overhead dropped five thousand vanda orchid blossoms. Another plane dropped a second load of orchids. It was quite a sight.

The crewmen lowered the coffin, and as it reached the water, Reverend Akaka led everyone in singing "Aloha Oe." And as the coffin began its slow descent into the sea, Nani and the children dropped leis in the water.

And then, as if on cue, the clouds gave way, revealing the sun in all its radiant glory.

As I reported in Jack Lord's chapter, Leonard Freeman, the creator, writer and producer of *Hawaii Five-O,* gave me his verbal approval to produce a film based on Kui's life. Lenny had also raised the film's financing. I was slated to be the writer and associate producer. He offered me a permanent position with his production company.

My dream had come true! I was ready to give up my newspaper career, to say "Aloha!" to the column business.

But first, Lenny had to check into the hospital for some minor surgery to fix a "stomach problem." Then, he assured me, he planned to produce *Kui.*

Then came the awful, devastating news: Lenny Freeman, in the prime of life, at age fifty-three, died on the operating table during heart surgery.

I was saddened for Lenny. At the same time, however, my dream was over.

Or so I thought.

For over half a century, Hal Wallis was one of the greatest

producers in Hollywood. He made film classics such as *Yankee Doodle Dandy* and *Casablanca*. He had hundreds of productions in all, including *True Grit, Rooster Cogburn, The Maltese Falcon, Gunfight at the O.K. Corral* and many more. This was during the Golden Age of Hollywood.

Wallis painted a huge cinema canvas and covered many bases. He was able to segue from making major film classics to producing the silly, low-budget Martin and Lewis comedies and Elvis Presley moneymakers. Wallis was the first to think Elvis had film possibilities and quickly put him under contract after he saw Presley's screen test. He obviously had a keen sense of what it took for screen stardom.

Without question, Wallis was one of the major icons of the cinema world. Among his many discoveries who got their start through him were talents such as Kirk Douglas, Burt Lancaster, Bette Davis, Henry Fonda, Richard Burton, Humphrey Bogart and Charlton Heston.

Thus, you can understand my excitement when Wallis called and said he wanted to produce *Kui*. Hal Wallis producing a script that I wrote? Who could have dreamed of such a thing? I walked around in a daze for that entire day.

After that, for almost a year, I visited Hal at his home in Rancho Mirage or at his Hollywood offices. He was an excellent script doctor and made many good suggestions about *Kui*.

One special room in his Beverly Hills office suite contained a library of scripts that he either had the rights to or owned outright. Showing it off to me, he remarked, sweeping an arm across the room, "I can make almost any one of these I want."

I asked him the obvious question. "Then what do you like about *Kui*? Why do you think it'll make a good movie?"

He smiled. "It's the kind of love story I like," he said. "And it's about a rebel, the underdog who fights his way out of his situation. Plus, Kui was a person of tremendous talent and wonderful music. Besides, it offers a nice opportunity for me to work in Hawaii. I always had such a good time making Elvis' movies there."

As the months and visits rolled by, I began to get the feeling that

Wallis' time as a major motion picture producer might have come and gone. The fire and desire were still there, but age seemed to have diminished his energy. He was still conveying the image of producer. His office appeared to be busy. When I was there, the phone continued to ring. His secretary acted as if there were all sorts of projects in the works. But, in actuality, nothing was really happening.

However, he loved to talk about his halcyon days as the "King of Hollywood." And that he truly was.

Although Wallis seemed to enjoy traveling down memory lane, he was bitter about some of the stars that he discovered.

"I found actors that I thought had great potential and gave them the opportunity to shine," he said. "And in return, many turned out to be just selfish ingrates."

One he talked disparagingly about was Shirley MacLaine. He discovered her in the Broadway hit *Pajama Game*.

Carol Haney was the show's star, and the production opened to rave reviews. After a short run, however, Haney hurt her ankle, and understudy MacLaine took over the role. It just so happened Wallis was in the audience on the very first night MacLaine played the lead.

Wallis was so impressed with her performance that he visited MacLaine backstage after the show and, of course, signed her to a contract. Just like that, she was off to fame and fortune.

However, it was a rocky road for this dynamic young actress. Eventually, she bought out her contract with Wallis—it took years to do it—and was quite critical of him afterward. She regarded her years under contract to Wallis as slavery. He answered by saying that, if that was so, she was quite handsomely compensated for her "slavery."

In his autobiography, *Ragman's Son*, Kirk Douglas remembers Wallis as taciturn and remote. When Wallis heard that Douglas and Burt Lancaster (two of his "finds") had become fast friends and would stay up talking till all hours of the night after working all day, Wallis asked Kirk what they could possibly talk about for so long. "How sad that Hal Wallis who was able to pick stars, including me and Burt, had no real friends who he could hold lengthy conversations with," Douglas wrote.

About the time Hal and I were talking about *Kui* in 1981, he had a bad auto accident in Palm Springs and was hospitalized. More misfortune followed. Because of diabetes, something he thought he had under control, his toes and left foot were amputated.

I returned to Hawaii in 1985. A year later, Hal Wallis was gone.

Fast Fact: Kui Lee

Upon returning to Hawaii in 1961, Kui Lee became a doorman and part-time performer at Honey's in Kaneohe, the nightclub that ultimately launched the career of singer Don Ho.

NINETEEN

Larry Mehau

When an important dignitary from the Mainland or a foreign country traveled to Hawaii in the 1960s, Larry Mehau was almost always assigned as driver and bodyguard. He provided these services for Presidents John Kennedy, Lyndon Johnson and Richard Nixon, among many others.

While driving for Johnson, for instance, Larry was asked by LBJ to "lose" the escorting parade of cars. The President apparently wanted to have some fun. Larry quickly zoomed off and was at the designated residence before everybody else could catch up. According to Larry, LBJ seemed to enjoy the little "chase."

In Hawaii, Larry Mehau became something of a celebrity in his own right. In January 1995, *MidWeek* featured a cover story on Larry and followed that with another feature the next week. Few personalities ever received that kind of coverage in the popular local magazine.

At that time, Larry was a very controversial figure. He had been investigated by just about every local and national law enforcement agency you can think of. They were all looking for any evidence to validate rumors that he was Hawaii's godfather of crime. They all struck out. Not a single shred of evidence was found implicating Larry in any way.

In the early 1970s, when Governor John Burns was serving his last term and battling cancer at the same time, he held a private meeting with a friend in the back storeroom of the M & M Country Store in Waimea, on the Big Island. He told his friend about his dreams for Hawaii's future, and asked for his help and support for Burns' political heir and protege, George Ariyoshi.

That friend was Larry Mehau. There was only one other witness to that meeting on a cool, sunny afternoon in rural Waimea: me.

Because of that promise, Larry demonstrated in the ensuing years his unique talent for organizational politics. That's why, I believe, he was targeted by political enemies. For years, the rumors persisted that Larry was involved with organized crime in Hawaii. The loud whispers were that the Honolulu Police Department kept files on him.

The truth of the matter is that Larry indeed knows about Hawaii's criminal element. And, yes, he does have a record on file with the police.

Like former Governor Burns, Larry Mehau was an ex-cop. He began his police career in 1953 as a patrolman. From there, he was assigned to the Morals Squad. He then moved to the Gambling Squad, then the Metro Squad. Over the years, he developed an incredible network of informants. Many of them were in the underworld.

During his Metro years, Larry organized and trained one of the best squads in the history of Honolulu's police force. Dressed in civilian clothes, Larry's specially selected crime fighting officers drove the city streets in unmarked cars looking for trouble, usually finding it and dealing quickly with offenders. His team was physically and mentally tough. They carved out an enviable record. The legend of Larry Mehau began, and his success bred respect and, unfortunately, envy.

During my early days as a newspaper columnist for the *Honolulu Advertiser*, I often accompanied Larry on his nightly crime-busting forays. I marveled at his fearlessness, his incredible strength when tested by the punks of Honolulu's underbelly, and his keen understanding of the criminal mind. It was quite obvious that Larry was not just another cop. He had a special talent. His superiors on the police force recognized this and moved him up the ladder with promotion after promotion.

One night, as Larry and I cruised along Hotel Street, I noticed a heavily muscled dude walking along, snarling at passersby while he pounded half of a pool cue into his hand. It was obviously a formidable weapon. Larry was looking in another direction as we drove past, but when I told him about the guy, he spun the car around the block, quicly spotted him and stopped about ten feet away. He got out of the car, extended his hand to this mean-looking character and said quietly, "Police officer, hand over the stick."

The guy hissed, "Come and get it."

I must've blinked for just a second because when I looked again the troublemaker was flat on his back, with Larry's knee on his throat. Larry told him he was going to drive around the block one more time, and if he saw the guy again he'd arrest him. I learned that Larry's tactics were to administer justice quickly and fairly. It was quite an eye-opener.

Some of Hollywood's best and brightest also got to ride on patrol during Larry's days with the Metro Squad, including Marlon Brando, Bob Conrad, Burgess Meredith and Bob Cummings.

Often when things were a little slow on patrol, Larry would take me to a construction yard and teach me how to break bricks with my hands and even my head. When I mentioned this to my compatriots at the paper, they didn't believe me. So a demonstration was set up on the roof of the *Advertiser*. The next day, the paper ran a series of pictures of me smashing the bricks bare-handed.

Once, when I was asked to emcee a 19-hour March of Dimes telethon at Farrington High School, I enlisted Larry's assistance on security. He was it—the entire security force. Many local entertainers also came by to lend their talents to the cause, and the 19 hours sped by.

The March of Dimes people also had a group of tough motorcycle riders constantly riding around the city, picking up people's pledges. To kill some time during a slow period in the wee hours of the morning, I asked the bikers if any of them could tear a phone book in half. I invited them up on stage to try their luck. One by one these beefy young lads grunted and groaned, trying to rip the phone book. None succeeded.

Eventually, I decided to "try" my luck. Then, in front of the TV audience and the motorcycle gang, I tore the book in half. It only took me a few seconds.

The biker boys were aghast. They were younger and stronger,

but I had showed them up. They were steaming. Hanging around backstage, they discussed "taking care of me" after the show. Mehau overheard them plotting. He walked over and issued a warning: attack Sherman and they'd answer to him. Of course, they all backed down, and the crisis was averted.

How did I do it? During those construction yard excursions, Larry had also instructed me on the "impossible"—how to tear a phone book in half. There was a trick to it. With lots of practice, I made it look easy. But it almost got me into a lot of trouble that night at Farrington High School.

Though he was almost always reluctant to talk about himself, Larry was also a master of various forms of martial arts, as well as sumo wrestling. At one time in the 1960s, he put together a special sumo team. An offer came from Japan to travel there and participate in sumo contests with other non-pros. Larry and his team triumphed, winning five out of six tournaments. As a result they were honored with a ticker tape parade in Tokyo.

His last assignment on the Honolulu police force was to head up the Canine Squad, training dogs and providing self-defense instruction to police recruits.

Larry was still a young man when a hand injury forced him to retire from the force. He decided he wanted to be a rancher. In 1963, through The Hawaiian Homes Commission, he had acquired 300 acres of ranch land in Waimea on the Big Island. So Larry, his wife, Beverly, and their five young children left behind the comforts of modern Honolulu to find a new life on the ranch.

Home was a small shack on the top of a knoll of his new "estate." His rickety house had only a few rooms and was sparsely furnished. There was no electricity, no telephone, no TV—none of the modern conveniences that most of us take for granted. The Mehaus also had very little money. It would be many years before they would know and enjoy the pleasures of comfortable living. The life of a rancher was hard work. The hours were long. It was a primitive existence, but Larry loved it.

During those lean, struggling years, he was often visited by people seeking special favors or help in solving problems that they couldn't handle themselves. People came from all areas of Island society—including those with ties to crime. Why? Simply, they knew of Larry's vast network of contacts made during his days on the police force. He possessed that rare combination of political know-how, negotiating ability and general street smarts. Larry gave everyone who came to him a hearing. If he believed he could help, and the request was justified, he lent his services. He never asked for anything in return.

One day, visiting Larry at his ranch, I asked him why he did what he did for so many people, often risking his life when he ventured into the criminal world.

"I really don't know," he laughed. "I just can't help it. If I feel that someone truly needs my help, deserves that kokua and has nobody to turn to, I will try. But only if I feel that the request is justified, honest and true."

Larry was once a big help to me. My then-ten-year-old son, Shawn, was having behavioral problems. After I told Larry about it, he suggested that I send him to the ranch for a bit of toughening up.

No question, the boy was a little spoiled. He balked at doing the ranch chores, picked at his food, and was not very cooperative or friendly. One day, one of Larry's sons put Shawn on a ranch pony. During the ride Shawn fell off the horse and was accidentally kicked. Crying, he ran after Larry.

Shawn pointed to the pony. "That horse kicked me," he sobbed.

Larry walked over and took the pony's reins and led him off as Shawn tagged along.

"What are you gonna do, Uncle Larry?" asked my son. "Are you going to spank him?"

"Worse than that," was Larry's reply.

"Hit him?"

"Worse than that, Shawn."

The boy was perplexed. What could be worse than being hit?

Larry suddenly stopped, picked the pony up, put it on its side, took out a knife and castrated the animal. Blood flew in all directions. My son stood there, dumbfounded.

Larry smiled. "He won't kick you anymore," he said.

Larry had planned to do the chore anyway, but he decided to put on a little show for the kid. Shawn's eyes bulged out of his head. He watched in shock. That night at dinner with the family, Shawn was again picking at his food when Larry commanded, "Shawn. Eat."

"Yes, sir, Uncle Larry!" exclaimed Shawn. He cleaned his plate in seconds. There were no more problems with the boy during the rest of his stay at the Mehau ranch.

Once, during a milk war in Honolulu, a telephone line repairman overheard a conversation while high up on the pole. Two men were plotting to set a bomb off at a milk company. When the company received the news, they reported it to the police. Because there was no evidence other than an alleged telephone conversation, the police were powerless to do anything. In desperation, the milk company contacted Larry, who acted swiftly.

Within hours, he had met with the two people who reportedly made the threat. Larry told them that if they carried out their intentions, he personally would suffer economic hardship because he wouldn't be able to sell milk from his ranch. And if that happened, he told them, he would be very upset. That was all Larry had to say. The message hit home with the culprits like an arrow splitting a bull's eye. The bombing never took place, and grateful milk company management heaved sighs of relief.

Another time, when Mainland criminal elements wanted a piece of Don Ho's success in Waikiki, the worried entertainer contacted Larry. The Mainlanders came to town, but their stay was short after a meeting with Larry. He convinced them that it would be very unwise to linger too long in Hawaii's sunshine. They got the message and were on a plane back to the Mainland that very same day.

To supplement his initially meager ranching income, Larry started the Hawaii Protective Agency, providing security services for businesses. The agency prospered. The word around town was: if you need help and can't get it, see Larry Mehau. His legend grew. And so did his political influence. He became one of Governor Ariyoshi's closest confidants.

During the 1978 governor's race, Ariyoshi was at one point many percentage points behind his challenger. He looked to be a sure loser. Larry decided to stage a giant political rally at Aloha Stadium. The numbers for the event were staggering: hundreds of volunteers, thousands of plates of food, and entertainers galore. Larry pulled out all the stops in organizing the event. But one local show business personality refused to be involved because it was a political rally.

"Well," said Larry, "if that's your decision, so be it. But please, in the future, don't ask me to do you another favor like the last time you had a problem." The entertainer quickly changed his mind and agreed to do the show, but Larry refused his services.

The Ariyoshi rally drew more than 50,000 people—the largest of its kind in Hawaii's history. There's no question it helped Governor Ariyoshi get re-elected. Naturally, political opponents were quick to capitalize on the Mehau association. Rumors flew that many entertainers were threatened with bodily harm if they did not perform. The falsehood brigade had a field day. All the accusations led up a blind alley and, eventually, the furor abated.

However, the Mehau mystique grew.

In various conversations I've had with people, they've often said that there must be something to all the stories about Larry. Where there's smoke, they said, there's fire. Most believed what they read, especially when accusations were leveled at Larry by officials in public office. After all, these officials must know something; they must have some kind of proof. If not, why would they say such things?

If a lie is told often enough, it sometimes becomes accepted as fact. Millions of people believed Hitler. In our own country, millions believed Senator Joe McCarthy during his anti-communist crusade. It is my belief that the chief reason Larry was a target for some overzealous public officials was because of his behind-the-scenes political success. Why? Simple. Get Larry, and the Governor he had helped would become tainted. And whoever succeeded in this endeavor could become a political hero.

Eventually, Larry was vindicated of all the vicious rumors and accusations by those who labeled him a crime lord. If Larry Mehau was what his enemies claimed, I certainly have not seen one iota of it in knowing the man and his family for more than forty years.

Fast Fact: Larry Mehau

Larry Mehau loves plants, big and small. His Big Island ranch is a landscaping showplace, and he is also an expert in the delicate art of bonsai.

TWENTY

Lenny Bruce

It isn't often that you're privileged enough to meet someone in show business (or any other profession) and have the distinct feeling that you're in the presence of future greatness. Call it instinct.

I felt that certain "tingle" while observing one particular entertainer in Honolulu. It was 1956. A year earlier, I had become a columnist for the *Honolulu Advertiser*, and my primary beat was show biz. And appearing at the Orchid Room atop the Waikiki Tavern was a comic by the name of Lenny Bruce.

Lenny was a good-looking young man. Offstage, he was a quiet sort, but still quick with a quip and possessing a likable, friendly quality. At the time, other than some traditional Hawaiian shows, there wasn't that much activity on Honolulu's after-dark entertainment scene. Certainly, there wasn't a comic like Lenny.

I visited the Orchid Room often, sometimes with J. Akuhead Pupule, who was fast becoming Hawaii's most popular early morning radio personality. What fun those days were! We all enjoyed each other's company, staying up till the wee hours and sharing the show business stories that we all loved.

I was only a few years removed from my own stand-up career on the East Coast. Comics like Lenny proliferated. Most "borrowed" material from the more successful comedians. Lenny, however, had started to write some original comedy that he slowly began injecting into his act, which at the time was a basic, standard, small-time presentation of jokes, impressions and song.

One night at the Orchid Room, the audience was exceptionally enthusiastic and gave Lenny a standing ovation. I stood along with them. He returned for another curtain call, but this time he was stark naked! Only a derby covered his privates. As he stood there, basking in the applause, he started egging on the crowd.

"More?" he asked.

Of course, he got another rousing ovation. And with that, Lenny spread his arms out wide, exposed his private parts and yelled, "Taa-dahh!"

Now, that took balls. Literally.

Lenny was married to a stripper—a beautiful, curvaceous redhead named Honey Harlow. Around that time, Honey was arrested for possession of marijuana and was put on three years probation. In 1957, Honey and Lenny divorced, and Lenny got custody of their fourteen-month-old daughter. Later that year, Honey was transferred to a Mainland prison to serve out the remainder of her sentence. She later returned to Honolulu and opened a small business. She passed away in Hawaii in 2005.

Lenny returned to Honolulu in September 1962 to play the Clouds Nightclub on Kapahulu Avenue, right across from the Honolulu Zoo. But this was a far cry from the Lenny Bruce who had appeared at the Orchid Room six years earlier. Now dressed in a Nehru jacket, he had dramatically expanded his style and subject matter. His act was laced with profanity, practically unheard of in clubs at that time. He was definitely overstepping the bounds of what was considered in the 1950s and '60s to be "respectable."

Lenny was fresh and daring, breaking almost every comedic rule there was. I admit, I could not relate to his material. Being an admirer of the great comics of stage, screen, and vaudeville, I basically agreed with people like Bill Cosby and Red Skelton, who said you don't need to be dirty to get laughs.

I did appreciate his willingness to be original, however.

After one of his Clouds shows, we adjourned to a nearby restaurant and reminisced about his days at the Orchid Room.

"It's a totally different show biz for me now," he said. "All the old, corny shit is gone, man. It's over. I'm more into spontaneity and free association. I feel like a musician. I just go out there and blow my horn. Whatever comes into my head comes out of my mouth. I talk about what I feel like talking about. Nothing pre-planned. No script. True, I use a lot of profanity. But they're just words, man. What can they hurt? And for that they arrest me. Is that crazy?"

Lenny's arrests became almost routine. Police officers were lined up at the back of the clubs, waiting for him to drop an obscenity. And believe me, they didn't have to wait long. The minute it happened, Lenny was hauled off the stage, cuffed and deposited in jail.

In later performances, he put his encounters with the police into his comedy routines. His act also included rants about court battles over his obscenity charges, tirades against fascism and the denial of his free speech. Predictably, this only caused the police to increase their harassment. He was banned outright from several cities and even entire countries, including Australia and England. By 1966, he was blacklisted by nearly every nightclub in America because the owners feared being prosecuted for obscenity.

In spite of all the pressures and turmoil in his life, Lenny refused to clean up his language. Interestingly enough, after he was arrested in New York in 1964, Norman Mailer, James Jones and other prominent writers and intellectuals began defending him as a social satirist.

As time went on and his troubles compounded, Lenny became addicted to heroin, and he began to slide into oblivion. Clubs refused to book him. A widely publicized six-month court trial found him guilty of obscenity charges in 1964, and Lenny was sentenced to four months in the workhouse.

While free on bail, he died of a drug overdose. His conviction was eventually overturned by a New York Court of Appeals in 1970. In time, New York Governor George Pataki pardoned him.

Many of today's comedians whose acts consists of liberal use of profanity—and that's a long list, from Eddie Murphy to George Carlin—freely admit that it was Lenny Bruce who paved the way for them. He suffered mightily for it. Thanks to many books, albums and a film based on his life starring Dustin Hoffman, Lenny has become a one-of-a-kind legend. An original.

Lenny Bruce was found dead in the bathroom of his Hollywood Hills home, lying naked with a pair of trousers around his ankles. A syringe and burned bottle cap were found nearby, along with various other narcotics paraphernalia. He was only forty years old. Now *that's* obscene.

After his death, one of New York's prosecutors, Assistant District Attorney Vincent Cuccia, expressed regret over his role in the case.

"I feel terrible about Bruce," he said. "We drove him into poverty and bankruptcy, and then murdered him. We used the law to kill him."

Fast Fact: Lenny Bruce

Lenny Bruce got his first big break as a guest on the TV show *Arthur Godfrey's Talent Scouts*, doing impressions of famous movie stars. The bit received only a lukewarm reception, and Bruce decided to take his act in a different direction.

TWENTY-ONE

Marlon Brando

When I first met Marlon Brando in 1956, he was at the very peak of his career—the bright, shining golden boy of Hollywood and the New York stage. He was widely acclaimed as the greatest actor of his day.

Jack Cummings, a producer at MGM and a nephew of the famed and legendary studio boss Louis B. Mayer, set up our meeting. At that time, besides my newspaper work, I was hosting a daily radio show over at KGU from the Moana Hotel's coffee shop. It was a program of my own creation called "Breakfast at Waikiki." Basically, the show consisted of interviews with visiting celebrities and games with the audience. I had interviewed Cummings a few times, and we became friendly, going to dinners and seeing the sights.

Cummings was producing *Teahouse of the August Moon*, starring Brando. During one of their stops in Honolulu, I met the star briefly.

Weeks later, when Brando was flying to Honolulu from Japan, Cummings called me from Los Angeles and asked if I'd go to the airport, meet Brando and offer any assistance he needed.

When I arrived at the terminal of the old John Rodgers Airport on Lagoon Drive, I noticed the familiar face of an ex-Honolulu wrestler nearby. Only a few other people were standing around. This was long before bustling Honolulu International Airport was built.

In those days, passengers could walk down the stairs from the aircraft to a waiting car or taxi near the sidewalk. When I asked the former wrestler who he was meeting, his response was, "Marlon Brando. I'm taking him to my hotel."

Knowing Cummings wouldn't have made additional arrangements for Brando unless informing me, I smelled something fishy. Further questioning uncovered the man's intentions. He didn't know the movie star, but had learned of his pending arrival. Furthermore, no one had asked him to meet the actor. He was simply determined to get Brando to his hotel, to help put the establishment on the map.

When Brando arrived, the ex-wrestler quickly ran over and introduced himself. Grabbing Brando's luggage, he began walking him to his limo. I was leaning against a nearby coconut tree, observing the entire scene.

The next part of the conversation between Brando and the ex-wrestler went something like this.

Brando: "Where are you taking my bags?"

Ex-wrestler: "To my car."

Brando: "Did the studio send you?"

Ex-wrestler: "No."

Brando: "So, who are you?"

Ex-wrestler: "I manage a small hotel in Waikiki. And I want you to be my special guest."

Brando (softly but very firmly): "Take my bags out of the car, please."

The ex-wrestler took hold of Brando's arm and said, "It's okay. Just come with me."

Brando quickly twisted his arm out of the wrestler's grip. His jaw set and he angrily hissed between his teeth, "Goodbye."

It was right around this time that Brando noticed me. "What are you doing here?" he asked.

"Jack Cummings asked me to come out and meet you and offer any needed assistance," I said, smiling.

He nodded. "Got a car?"

I pointed to my beat-up jalopy. Brando quickly retrieved his luggage, and a couple of minutes later, I was chauffeuring him out of the airport.

"Where to?" I asked.

"Wherever you live," answered Brando.

At that time, I lived on Ala Wai Boulevard in Waikiki, in maybe the tallest building in the area at that time—a whopping three stories high! I shared a large apartment with two other bachelors. One was Flash Miller, then manager of Queen's Surf, one of the most popular nightclubs in Waikiki; the other was an unemployed engineer named Al Pellitier.

When we arrived at the apartment, Brando seemed to take an immediate liking to the place and asked about the possibility of renting a unit in the building for a few weeks. He liked the building because it was away from the major hotels and tourist hordes on the other side of Waikiki. In other words, it offered exactly what he wanted: privacy.

Brando wound up renting the apartment across the hall, and that began my fifteen-year-long friendship with the actor. Every day during his stay, he wanted to go somewhere—a place to see, explore and experience.

He seemed curious about everything. And so I briefly became a tour guide and chauffeur for Hollywood's biggest star.

Whatever image I previously had of Brando was totally different from what he was like in person. He was extremely caring and polite. Whomever he met, he treated with courtesy and respect. He was so "un-movie-star-like." No airs or ego. Very down to earth, with a charming and sly sense of humor.

He seldom talked about himself, or his career. He was always interested in other people. If he met someone he especially liked, he quietly "interviewed" him or her as though he were a newspaper reporter.

One morning, he came over to the apartment for the day's itinerary.

"Gotta visit my doctor," I said. "He's in the hospital with a stroke. I don't think he's gonna make it."

"Can I go too?" he asked.

On the way to the hospital, I told Brando this story about Doctor Bob Ruff.

Every weekend, a group of single men and women met on the

beach near the Moana Hotel for camaraderie, games, gossiping and just plain socializing. Bob Ruff was one of the crowd.

One day, knowing Bob was a young medic, I complained about a pain in my side. He felt the area. "You have a hernia," he told me. "You better have an operation."

I explained that I didn't have medical insurance at the time, and couldn't afford it. "Don't worry," he said. "I'm just starting out in my practice, and I'll be happy to do it for you for free. I need the experience."

"Have you ever done the operation?" I asked.

"No," he answered. "But I know how it's done. Really, you have nothing to worry about."

So I checked into St. Francis Hospital in Honolulu. Bob performed the surgery, and all went well.

While I was in the hospital recuperating, I told this story to my nurse. I talked about how kind Dr. Ruff was to do all this for free because he said he wanted more medical practice.

That caused the nurse to laugh. "Is that what he told you?" she said, giggling some more. "Dr. Ruff happens to be the head of surgery at St. Francis. He's one of the best doctors in Hawaii. This hospital tried to recruit him from a big Mainland medical facility for a the longest time, and we finally did it. You had a top-notch surgeon operate on you!"

On the way to the hospital, Brando spotted a florist shop and asked me to pull over. He came out with an armload of flowers. We entered Dr. Ruff's room, where he was sitting up in bed. When he saw Brando with the flowers, his jaw dropped and his eyes widened. For a few minutes, he seemed to be in shock. For over half an hour, Brando sat on the bed and plied Bob with questions about his condition, his career and the medical profession. The next day, Bob called and thanked me.

"It was one of the most thrilling experiences for me," he said. "What a wonderful human being he is. I'll never believe any of those nasty stories you see in the papers."

A few weeks later, Dr. Ruff died.

One of the things Brando and I had in common was a love of boxing. When he very young and starring on Broadway in *A Streetcar Named Desire*, Brando used to work out at Stillman's Gym, a famous New York hangout for professional fighters. He told me this story:

While Brando was going through his routine in the gym one day, Rocky Graziano approached. The future middleweight champ said he liked his style and asked if Marlon would like a few tips. That started a friendship.

Graziano had no idea Brando was anything other than an ambitious boxer. A few weeks later, while both were working out, Graziano asked Brando if he'd give him a ride to Broadway. Brando explained he only had a motorcycle, which, of course, was okay with the champ.

Arriving at the *Streetcar* theater, Brando explained this was where he worked and he had to go to rehearsal.

"What do you do here, kid?" asked Graziano.

Brando pointed to the theater marquee, where his name was spelled out in huge letters above the play's title. Rocky was impressed. Brando said he'd leave a couple tickets for him at the box office whenever he wanted to see the show.

Weeks went by. The next time Brando was working out at Stillman's, Rocky approached. Grabbing Brando by the shoulder, he spun him around and shoved him against the wall.

"Hey, prick, I saw your play," the boxer growled. "And ya know what? In that show you talk just like me."

Brando sheepishly admitted he had based his characterization and verbal delivery of the Stanley Kowolski character on Rocky's personality.

Because we were both fight fans, eventually, over the course of Brando's many Hawaii visits, he and I developed a slow-motion boxing routine. It was just a gag, of course, with us making lots of faces, with grunts and groans. Looking back, we should have filmed it. It was quite funny.

The filming of the 1962 movie *Mutiny on the Bounty* in Tahiti was plagued with many problems, including being way over budget. Brando himself was blamed for most of the problems.

He was seething during one of his visits to Hawaii after the picture was completed. He was angry at everyone pointing the finger at him for the movie's failures.

After a particularly blistering *Saturday Evening Post* report on the subject, again making Brando the scapegoat of the whole project, he decided to file a multi-million-dollar suit against the magazine.

He asked if I would interview him on local TV because he wanted to talk about *Bounty* and tell his side of the story.

I pointed out that doing an interview on TV in Honolulu was like tossing a pebble into a large pond. It wouldn't reach much of an audience. He could easily go on national television instead and hit millions of viewers.

However, he insisted on doing the interview here in Hawaii. With me.

Brando arrived at the studio wearing a white suit he had purchased just for the interview. It was as though he were getting ready for a special appearance on national TV.

I asked the station (KGMB) to use only a black background, and to turn the red lights on the cameras off, so we wouldn't know where they were positioned during the telecast. And, of course, I asked them to tape the program.

Brando and I faced each other. A small table between us held two cups of coffee. That was the set.

I opened with a simple, "Good evening, my special guest is Marlon Brando." Brando smiled and sipped the coffee. He paused, and then made a quizzical expression. Then he sipped his coffee again. Smiling at me, he softly said, "Eddie, there's no sugar in the coffee."

Realizing he was playing with me, I went along. Remember, we were live. So, I sipped my coffee and paused for a few seconds, then said, "Marlon?"

"Yes?" he said.

"There *is* sugar in the coffee."

This went on for just a couple of minutes, but it seemed like an eternity. Finally, he stopped the clowning and the interview began in earnest. He dodged no subject. He spoke eloquently, especially about his problems with *Mutiny on the Bounty*. In effect, the interview turned out great, very special, and I was grateful to have had a worldwide exclusive.

The next day I went to KGMB to buy a copy of the videotape. The manager said matter-of-factly, "Sorry, but we erased the show from the tape because we needed it to tape something else." I looked at him, dumbfounded. Was this a joke? Incredibly, it wasn't. This stupid son of a bitch actually erased the Marlon Brando interview that even today, after all these years, would have been some kind of a special. I think if I had a knife or a gun at that moment, I would have used it on that station manager. I was that overwhelmed with anger.

One of my favorite Marlon Brando stories involved my mother, Bessie. This was in 1960. After her second husband, Sam Robotnick, died, I asked her to come to Hawaii and live with me. Peggy Ryan, my wife at the time, was agreeable to the situation, and the arrangement worked out just fine. We took my mother to various functions, and she got to meet many famous people. Celebrities were captivated by Bessie's innocence, especially when they realized she had no idea who they were. They warmed up to her instantly.

It had been a long day at the *Advertiser*, and it ended with an interview with France Nuyen at the Hawaiian Village Hotel. France was then famous for playing the young love interest in the film *South Pacific*. In the middle of the interview, I had a call from Peggy. Our ten-year-old daughter, Kerry, had broken her arm after falling off a horse she was training. I told Peggy to send Kerry to Kaiser Hospital, which was then located next to the Village.

I ended the interview and rushed next door to the hospital. After setting her arm, the doctors decided she should remain in the hospital overnight. It was almost 11 p.m. when I got home.

Peggy was cooking our dinner when the phone rang.

It was Brando. "I just got in from Tahiti, and I'm hungry. Where can I get a good meal?" he asked.

I told him most of the better restaurants would probably be closed, but suggested he could eat with us if he wasn't too tired.

"Great," he said. "Pick me up."

Back I drove to the Hawaiian Village. When I came home and walked into our kitchen, Peggy had a hot meal, beef stew, just about ready. My mother was bent over trying to put a garbage bag in the pail when I introduced her to Brando.

She looked up, smiled, said hello, and continued with her garbage bag problem. Brando, ever sensitive to people's reactions to him, realized quickly that my mother had no idea who he was.

He loved it. This was a challenge. A chance to try to win her over. While my mother was struggling to get the bag in the pail, Brando stepped in. "Excuse me," he said. "You're doing it wrong."

My mother straightened up and put her hands on her hips. "Oh," she sighed, "you know from dis?"

"Of course," said Brando. "This is my business. I'm an expert at putting bags into garbage pails."

"Okay, mistah," said Bessie. "Show me."

Brando proceeded to "show" her. He ad-libbed a whole routine of double-talk, acting out special moves needed to properly install a garbage bag into a pail. "Tear it here, fold it there, tuck it in here." His act was priceless. We watched, holding back our laughter so as not to spoil the show. His routine lasted a good five minutes or more.

When he was finished, my mother thanked him, turned to me and said, "Such a nice, smart man."

Brando was happy. He had won her over.

The next evening, I had a function to attend. My mother and Peggy stayed home and watched *Saturday Night at the Movies*. The film shown that evening was *Desiree*, starring Marlon Brando. He played Napoleon. Throughout the picture, my mother kept squinting at the TV, remarking often to Peggy, "Dat man, he looks so familiar to me. I think I seen him someplace before."

Peggy didn't tell her who he was. When the movie was over, Peggy finally let the cat out of the bag. "That man," she said to Bessie, "was here last night. He really is a famous actor. His name is Marlon Brando."

Bessie was stunned. She exclaimed, "Dat's the garbage man?"

Yes, that was Bessie. It reminds me of a Harry Belafonte performance at the Waikiki Shell—Honolulu's answer to the Hollywood Bowl. That evening, my mother fell asleep during the first half of the show. But when Belafonte opened the second half with *Hava Nagila*, the popular Hebrew tune, she suddenly sat bolt upright, totally enraptured. She pounded her feet on the floor in rhythm with the song.

"I got to meet dat man!" she exclaimed.

Backstage after the show I had an opportunity to introduce Bessie to this great artist, whom I had interviewed a few days earlier. She gave him a warm smile, grabbed his forearm and gushed, "It's good to see a nice Jewish man like you doing so well." (He had to be Jewish, she thought, since he'd sung *Hava Nagila*.) Harry almost collapsed with laughter and gave her a big hug and kiss.

Another quick Bessie story: one night I introduced her to Dean Martin at a cocktail party. After they'd chatted for a minute or two, Dean asked her, "Who's your favorite singer?"

"Oh," my mother replied, "I just love Perry Coleman!"

Dean doubled over with laughter.

But back to Marlon Brando. For a number of years during his career, Brando was very involved in civil rights. He told me, "I've often thought of the possibility of making a film dealing with the untouchables in India. I think a film like that could provide some really useful perspective in areas where you find the most prejudice. Very often, the proximity of the problem keeps people from seeing the issues clearly.

"If this problem was presented from the view of others in India or the caste system you find among the Watusi in Africa, or the prejudice you find in Haiti, you'd see it's all the same. I think Americans would find it useful to see how other cultures handle prejudice, since it's a problem we all have in common. I've talked to many Indians and Pakistanis about the caste system, and I'd like to learn more.

"Of course, it's hard to get an idea of the real nature of a problem

A successful day of deep-sea fishing on the Kona Coast with Richard Boone.

Happy days: Lighter moments with France Nuyen...

...and long-time friend Larry Mehau.

HONOLULU STAR-BULLETIN

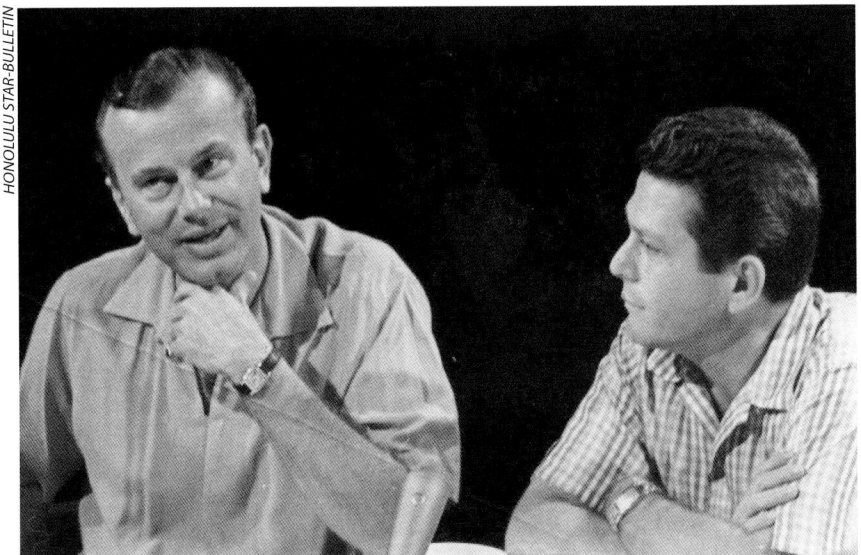

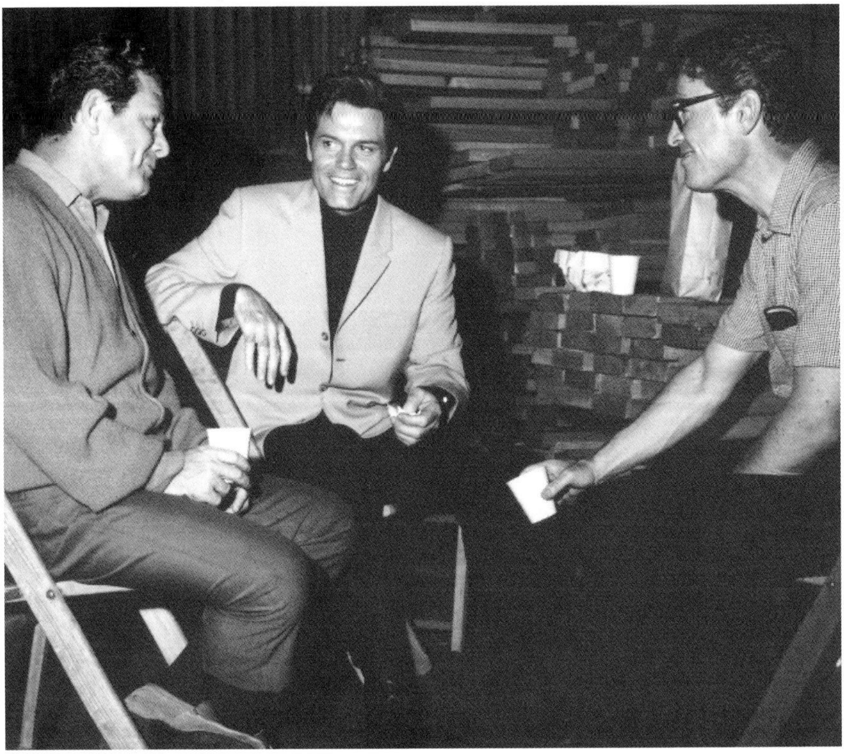

I share a *Five-O* scene with local newscaster Bob Sevey (*second from right*) and guest star Ricardo Montalban (*right*). *Opposite top*: Jack Paar rubbed local people the wrong way during the shows he filmed in Waikiki in 1961. *Opposite bottom*: A coffee break with *Hawaii Five-0* star Jack Lord (center) and producer Leonard Freeman.

Marlon Brando's love affair with Japan—and Japanese food—dated back to 1956 when he filmed *Sayonara* there. Here he enjoys the sushi at the Kyo-ya restaurant in Waikiki.

Wearing lavalavas, Brando and I do our slow-motion boxing routine on the beach at Waikiki.

The legendary Mervyn LeRoy produced or directed nearly 200 films, including *The Wizard of Oz* and *Devil at 4 O'Clock*, filmed on Maui. *Opposite*: In 1960 I visited Brando on the Paramount set of *One-Eyed Jacks*, which he both starred in and directed.

Milton Berle (below, *left*, with me and columnist Earl Wilson) came to the rescue when Red Skelton (*opposite*) fainted during Red's one-man show at the Waikiki Shell. *Bottom*: Another show-biz legend, Sammy Davis, Jr., hams it up at the old John Rodgers Airport in Honolulu.

Sugar Ray Robinson and I tied on the gloves and climbed into the ring—all in fun, of course. *Opposite top*: With Miiko Taka, who starred with Brando in *Sayonara*. *Opposite bottom*: Getting chummy with John Wayne and Burgess Meredith on the set of *In Harm's Way*.

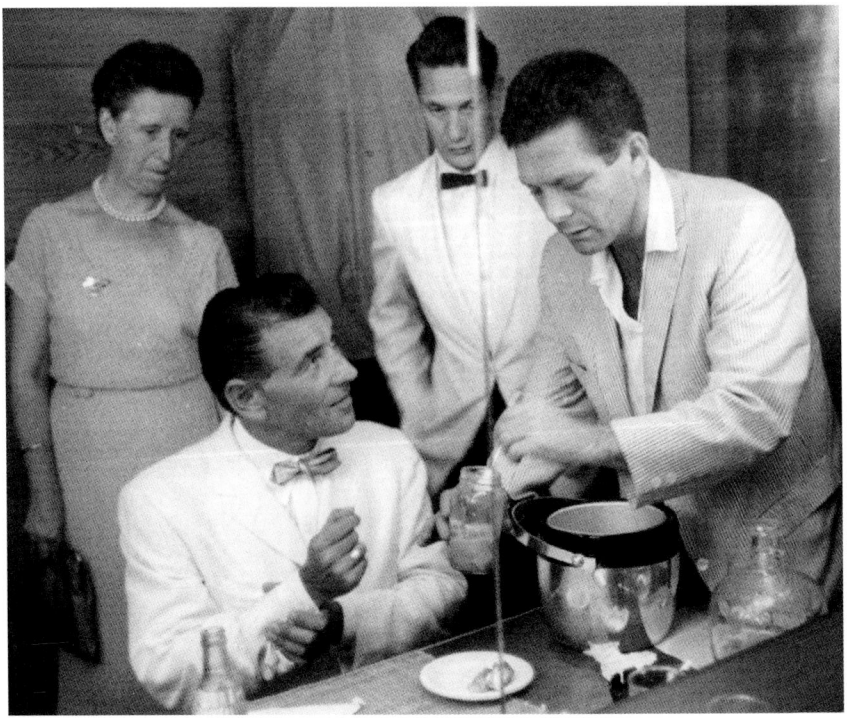

CAMERA HAWAII

Playing a little rope-a-dope with Muhammad Ali.
Opposite top: My wife, Patty, and I visit with Anthony Quinn.
Opposite bottom: I serve Leonard Bernstein my mother's pickled herring backstage at the Waikiki Shell.

At Hickam Air Force Base, I finally got to meet my three-dot idol, Walter Winchell.

without going to the country where it exists."

It was for this reason that he called on scholars at the East-West Center at the University of Hawaii, to get their point of view. "Since I can't go to India now, the next best thing to do is to have an exchange of views with the experts," Brando told me later.

Before leaving Hawaii, on that trip, he invited me to the Kyo-Ya restaurant in Waikiki so we could spend a quiet evening just talking. "We haven't had much of a chance to be alone since I've been here," he told me. "This way, nobody will interrupt us."

The restaurant's manager, Clara Morinaga, remembered what Brando had liked on a visit years earlier and prepared the menu in advance. One new dish, *shabu-shabu* (you cook the meat yourself by dipping it in water boiling in a copper bowl heated by charcoal), impressed Brando so much that Clara said she would send him a copper bowl as a gift.

One of the pretty waitresses serving us remarked how she enjoyed seeing Brando in the film, *Sayonara*. Setsuko Kotada asked in halting English if she could sing him the song from the film, which she did. Brando reciprocated by asking Setsuko if he could sing the most beautiful song he'd ever heard. She smiled and said, *"Prreeeze."*

Brando sang "Kimigayo," the Japanese national anthem.

Brando's love affair with Japan had begun when he went there in 1956 to make *Sayonara*. "I found the Japanese, without exaggeration, among the most refined of manner and certainly the most artistic people I've met," he told me. He went on and on about their harmonious integration of spiritual aspirations, artistic sensibility and their philosophical point of view about the menial aspects of everyday living.

In 1959, Brando had to cut a Hawaii visit short to make a Los Angeles court appearance. He and his former wife, Anna Kashfi, were in a legal battle over the custody of their son, Christian.

I was with him the day he was packing for the trip back to the Mainland. "Do you actually think a judge will give you custody with your track record as a parent?" I asked.

"Of course not," he said. "However, when I present my side of the story, maybe I'll be able to persuade the judge that she's not qualified to raise our son either. She's totally unfit. Boy, I could tell you stories! Of course, whatever problems we've had, I'm the one who's always blamed. What I really want is for the judge award custody to my sister, Jocelyn. She and her husband can raise him properly on their farm and give him a good home, totally away from my kind of life. He'll be so much better off. I know the press will give me a hard time—that I'm this and that. Okay, they'll knock the shit out of me. And crucify me. I don't care. I've got to get my son away from Anna."

What he wished for came true.

A picture of Anna Kashfi slapping Brando outside the courtroom circled the globe. Brando got his wish. The judge gave custody to his sister.

However, Christian Brando nevertheless grew into manhood a troubled person. He eventually went to jail for killing his sister's boyfriend.

Certainly, Marlon Brando was the most "unactorish" actor I've ever met. He told me, "Everything is really relative. I suppose being a movie star is the ultimate of success in the eyes of most. But it hasn't given me the happiness I've hoped for. However, I'm not blaming anyone but myself. Most of the trouble in my life has been my fault. I have stuck my chin out and said (pointing to his chin) 'Here, let me have it, right there.' And I'd get walloped.

"Today, I see things in a different perspective than I once did. I've learned that being honest with myself, admitting the truth no matter what the problem, is the only way. Too many people are quick to blame others and make excuses. If they would only face up to their problems, they'd find the going a lot easier."

On one occasion in 1962, in the wee hours of the morning, Brando and I were strolling along Beach Walk in Waikiki, chatting away, when suddenly I noticed he was no longer there beside me.

I turned around, and there was Brando peeing in the bushes.

Fortunately, the street was dimly lit and hardly anyone was

around. I walked over to him, took out my notebook and pen, and said, "'That big film star, Marlon Brando, was seen last night urinating in the bushes in Waikiki.' What the hell's the matter with you? You never heard of toilets? People will see you, and they'll be calling the papers. You could get arrested!"

He laughed, "I'm used to people looking at me. Besides, I had a bladder full. I had to piss real bad."

Although I never visited Brando on his Tahitian island, I did hear some very strange stories about him. One focused on a very unusual collection he reportedly kept. Whenever his world-famous friends visited him, he asked for samples of their bowel movements. He put them in bottles and had the contents labeled. Why he did that was never explained.

After Marlon Brando burst on the theatrical scene in New York with his spellbinding performance in *A Streetcar Named Desire*, it was a given that Hollywood was his next destination. A story he told me few know: when he first arrived on the West Coast, the William Morris Agency, which represented him, sent a mailroom clerk, Jay Cantor, to the airport to welcome him to Los Angeles. Apparently, the William Morris agents were all too busy to meet their new client from New York.

When Brando later sat down with the agency's executives to discuss which agent should represent him, he rejected them all. Instead, to everyone's shock and surprise, he chose the young man working in the mailroom who met him on his arrival in Los Angeles.

That was Jay Cantor's big break. As Brando's career flourished, Cantor eventually became a very important theatrical agent, and this brought him a flock of major actors as clients.

Of course, it didn't take long for Hollywood and the world of cinema to realize what an acting genius the young Marlon Brando was. In quick succession, he starred in a variety of different and spectacular roles that revealed his magnificent talents: *On the Waterfront, The Wild Ones, Viva Zapata!, Julius Caesar, One-Eyed Jacks* and, of course, *Mutiny on the Bounty*. Brando brought a new style of acting to the screen that would be copied by almost every actor in films, or so it seemed. Even today, the Brando influence in acting continues. So many young actors copy his technique. His influence was profound.

In short order, Marlon Brando became the new king of Hollywood.

He once told me that when he became a famous actor, people expected him to be an expert on everything: politics, government, world affairs, science and all sorts of other subjects. Because of his sense of humor, he sometimes went along with the media, giving seemingly authoritative interviews that had absolutely no credibility whatsoever. It was just a bunch of double-talk on any subject about which they asked his opinion. Often, reporters came away from those interviews amazed at his seemingly vast knowledge, but in most cases not knowing what the hell he was talking about.

Of course, neither did Brando.

Reporting on his death in 2004 at age of eighty, the Associated Press noted that he was often called the greatest actor of his time: "He created a naturalism that was sometimes derided for its mumbling, grungy attitudes. But audiences were electrified, and a new generation of actors adopted his style. Watching some of the top dramatic TV series today, you'll see quite a few leading actors doing their Brando, mumbling their lines.

"His impact on the screen was demonstrated by Academy nominations as best actor in four successive years for: *A Streetcar Named Desire*, the Mexican revolutionary in *Viva Zapata!*, as Marc Anthony in *Julius Caesar*, and as Terry Malloy in *On the Waterfront*. The latter garnered him his first Oscar.

"His image was a studio's nightmare. Millions of words have been written about his weight, his many marriages, his battle with producers and directors, and his refuge on the Tahitian island he purchased and frequently escaped to. Brando's career was reborn in 1972 with his brilliant and memorable depiction of the Mafia chieftain Don Corleone in Francis Coppola's *The Godfather*. It's considered one of the classics of all time. Critics and fans called it one of the greatest pieces of acting ever seen, and the film continues to play over and over again on TV.

"Brando created a character that will live for generations to come."

One more Brando story: one day in 1965, *Honolulu Advertiser* editor George Chaplin called me into his office. "Eddie, you and Brando have been seen all over Honolulu this week. Yet I don't see one word about him in your columns reporting any of this. It's one thing to be his friend, but you are also a columnist. So please do your job."

I told Brando the paper needed a story about him. He sat down, grabbed a pen and wrote out a dissertation about his travels in Asia. Just like that. After he read it, he decided he didn't like a particular paragraph, so he crossed it out and asked me to make sure it didn't get published.

It was deadline time when I turned the story in. I told the city desk to make sure that the paragraph crossed out in the story was not to be printed. And then I left to meet him at his hotel. The next day, the story he wrote ran in my column—including the paragraph he crossed out and did not want published.

I was furious! I knew what Brando's reaction would be, and I was right.

Brando didn't talk to me for the next two years.

He felt double-crossed, and under those circumstances, he was unforgiving. He told me how people had double-crossed him one way or another his whole life, and when it happened, that was the end of the relationship. Even though I explained my circumstances and why it happened, it fell on deaf ears. Nothing I said could make him change his mind. As far as he was concerned, I had stabbed him in the back, and that was that.

I feel privileged to have known Marlon Brando and cherished the close friendship we shared for many years. I found him to be kind, considerate and caring for his fellow man. And I appreciated and enjoyed his (hidden) sense of humor. Knowing him made me feel very special.

Upon his death on July 1, 2004, I think columnist Liz Smith best summed up his life. She said: "For whatever reason, I think he had a tragic life. He seemed unable to reconcile his talent, his instant myth, the demands of a disciplined career, his self-effacing sensitivity and giant ego. He made a mess of his personal life, and even there he projected a clueless astonishment through those troubles.

"And guilt. He was not a good father. He admitted this during the murder trial of his son, Christian.

"But, Brando managed to live until eighty and saw himself lionized as an iconic figure, and an example of wasted talent. One wonders which—if either—view he thought was true. The best of his work will live as long as the art of cinema. Fame Conquers Death—that is the theme of a great Medieval tapestry which hangs in the Metropolitan Museum of Art. It was true before the advent of the printing press, and it remains true today.

"Brando is now free of his conflicts and spared, one hopes, of watching his heirs—nine children—battle for his worldly goods."

Fast Fact: Marlon Brando

Marlon Brando portrayed Superman's father, Jor-El, in the 1978 box office hit *Superman*. He agreed to the role on the condition that he did not have to read the script beforehand. His lines were displayed somewhere off-screen.

TWENTY-TWO

Marty Rackin

Have you ever met someone with whom you felt an instant rapport? It's rare, I know, but it happens. That's how I felt the first time I met Marty Rackin, who was then head of Paramount Studios. It was as though we'd known each other forever.

He was in Honolulu in the early 1970s to visit his friends, Duke Kahanamoku and his wife, Nadine. He and I met over lunch. Marty reminded me of guys I grew up with in Boston. Fellas I used to hang around with in pool halls—down to earth, unpretentious and absolutely gregarious. Marty was just a funny and forward individual with movie-star looks. He easily could have passed for an actor.

One reason for our mutual attraction, I believe, was our involvement in journalism. As a youngster in New York, Marty became acquainted with the legendary writer and reporter Damon Runyon, and this led him to a job as copy boy for the *New York Mirror* and sort of a go-fer for Runyon. Eventually, Marty became an assistant nightclub columnist.

Although I had never met Runyon (he died in 1946 of throat cancer), I read his books and saw the numerous films based on his popular stories. I was a big fan. When I spent time with Walter Winchell, the most famous columnist of his day, Winchell told me a number of stories about the legendary Runyon. And I related Winchell tales to Rackin. Winchell and Runyon were inseparable. For years, the two roamed the New York canyons, chronicling their various beats.

Runyon was among the first to stylize both the language and the behavior of gangsters and focus on their specific characterizations.

He showed how the underworld provided clients with gambling, sex and even hard-to-get sports tickets—especially during the Prohibition years. Those wonderful characters in the Broadway and film musical *Guys and Dolls* were based on Runyon's high-spirited and often hilarious New York stories. Even today, you can see traces of his characters in various gangster films and TV shows such as *The Godfather* and *The Sopranos*.

Marty told me that any time I was in Los Angeles, I'd better call him—"Or else," he said with a laugh, "it's your ass, pal!" During one of those quick visits in the early 1970s, I just had a few hours left before boarding a plane back to Honolulu. I called him from a pay phone. His secretary told me that he couldn't be disturbed because he was in very important meetings with New York VIPs. I explained that he made me promise to call him, and that I was calling from a pay phone. I gave her my name and she asked me to hold on.

A few seconds later, Marty was on the phone.

"Hey, schmuck, where the hell are you?"

I told him I was calling from a pay phone in Beverly Hills and was leaving for Honolulu in a few hours. It was almost noon.

"Let's have lunch," he said. "Take a taxi to Canter's" (a famous deli). He cancelled the rest of his appointments for the next few hours, and we just swapped stories like two old buddies.

Rackin spent the rest of his screen career as an independent producer. He visited Honolulu often, and we discussed several potential film projects that could be made in Hawaii. However, none came to fruition. He died of a heart attack during a business trip to London in the 1970s, four years after his final production, *Two Mules for Sister Sara*.

Fast Fact: Marty Rackin

During a stint as a contract screenwriter for MGM, Marty Rackin wrote for comedian Red Skelton. He later produced and directed Skelton's TV show in the 1950s.

TWENTY-THREE

MAX WINTER AND FRIENDS

When Max Winter came to America from Austria at the age of ten, his father was a door-to-door fruit peddler. Max earned his keep selling papers on the streets of Minneapolis.

I first met the Winters in the mid-1950s, when I had just started my newspaper career. Max and his wife, Helen, were already firmly established as part-time residents of Honolulu. After the professional football season on the Mainland was over, they packed their bags and headed for their Diamond Head home for months of sunshine, balmy breezes and much-needed relaxation. In all, they were Hawaii residents for more than forty years.

Max, I quickly learned, was a major-league showman. He was president of the Minnesota Vikings football team and manager of the Minneapolis Lakers basketball team. He also promoted boxing, auto shows and the world-famous Harlem Globetrotters. Max also owned laundromats along the West Coast and in Alaska, several parking lots, a multi-million-dollar development company, a billboard business, a chain of restaurants, and a Waikiki boutique hotel, to name just a "few" of his enterprises.

It didn't take long for us to become fast friends. For many years, I often started my day with a stop at the Winters' residence, which overlooked Doris Duke's Diamond Head estate, for morning coffee and a long chat with Max. He was loaded with stories, and I was an eager listener.

Max had definite ideas about how Hawaii could compete better with other resort tourist destinations. "On the Mainland," he'd say to me, "everyone I talk to about this agrees that Hawaii has the beauty and climate, of course, but not enough activities. Not only a better entertainment picture, but also attractions like horse and dog racing. If that ever happened, the tourist industry would flourish beyond anyone's imagination. They say such events like that bring in the wrong crowd, but I don't believe it.

"As a matter of fact, nothing but good could come from this. States that have these racing activities realize thousands of tax dollars, and huge employment. Everyone benefits. Let's face it: tourists come here to spend money and have a good time. They've already seen most of the local attractions and ache for something new and different. But I don't think I'll live long enough to see any of this happen." (He was right.)

A millionaire many times over, Max was a very generous man. But he bristled if he believed someone was trying to take advantage of him, no matter how slight the perceived offense. Let me illustrate.

Max and Helen were in the mood one day for blintzes. So I took them to a deli that served the crepe-like delicacy near the Varsity Theater in Honolulu. When the dish arrived, it included the sour cream, but the traditional jam had been omitted. Max asked why there was no jam. The waitress replied, "Because it's twenty-five cents extra." Max informed her that jam is always served with the dish and that he could afford the twenty-five cents. She just shrugged and grunted. Furious, Max paid the bill, left a generous tip and stormed out, vowing never to return. (Note: Not too long after that, the deli folded. The jerk owner moved to another location, got into another "jam," stiffed a long list of vendors and then skipped town. Losers always lose.)

During all the years I spent with Max, I never saw him out of "uniform." His dress code in Hawaii was absolutely consistent: shorts and aloha shirt. His time in the Islands was mostly spent in the workshop that he built for himself in his garage. Max loved to tinker and fix things.

For fun and leisure, he usually headed to the Waialae Country Club, located a mile or so down the road from his home, for a little golf and gossip with his club cronies. He often entertained visiting guests and held many of his football meetings in Honolulu.

In 1968, Max invited me to watch his Minnesota Vikings play in Los Angeles. I had never seen a professional football game. He asked me to meet him in the hotel lobby, and at first, I had a hard time finding him. I guess I was looking for a guy in aloha shirt and shorts. I hardly recognized Max when I finally spotted him. He was holding court surrounded by a small group of people. It was a Max Winter I hadn't seen before: he was dressed in a neatly pressed blue suit, white shirt and flashy tie. He was the epitome of sartorial splendor.

Before the game, Max stationed himself near the players' entrance at the stadium, greeting all the athletes, dignitaries and other personnel as they trooped by. Finally, he said, "Okay, let's go in."

Unbelievably, the burly guard at the gate asked Max for his tickets.

Winter looked through his pockets. He couldn't find his tickets.

"But I own the Minnesota Vikings," Max pleaded. Watching the scene unfold, I had a hard time stifling my laughter.

The guard just shrugged, "Sorry, buddy. No ticket, you don't get in."

Finally, the stadium manager came by and rescued Max from the embarrassing situation. Winter, of course, realized the guard was just doing his job. He patted the guard on the back, slipped him a generous tip and said, "Good job, young man."

If you want to see a professional football game, you can't do better than sitting with the team's owner in the team's private quarters, high above the stadium. There's luxury and comfort deluxe, great spirits and all the gourmet food you can eat. In other words, you're treated like a king. Yes, it's good to be king, even if it's just for one Sunday afternoon.

Rewind to just a few years earlier. Dropping by Max's house one morning, I saw that he had two guests over for breakfast. My jaw dropped when he introduced me to the legendary Jack Dempsey, one of the greatest heavyweight champions in boxing history.

His other guest was almost as famous. It was Clyde Beatty, the fearless, world-renowned animal trainer.

Dempsey and Beatty were among my childhood heroes. Growing up, in fact, I read every book or magazine I could get my hands on about Dempsey. I saw films of many of his old fights. And, of course, I always looked forward to going to the Saturday matinee movies whenever a Clyde Beatty serial was playing. What a thrill it was to witness the greatest of all animal trainers fighting off lions and tigers.

To this day, meeting Dempsey and Beatty on that morning is one of the most memorable events of my life. Both men were very gracious and polite as I asked the same questions they've been asked their whole careers.

Beatty was born in 1903 and left home at age fifteen to work as a cage boy and acrobat for three dollars a week. It took him years to learn how to be a wild animal trainer. It was hard work but, little by little over the years, he developed one of the most successful "fighting acts" in the circus business. Beatty would enter a cage carrying a whip, a chair and a .38-caliber blank pistol. It was an aggressive display, and a sensational spectacle.

"I tried to make it look much easier than it was," he told me. "I paid a price, often getting clawed by the cats, and sometimes pretty seriously. But I loved the life."

At one time in the early 1950s, Beatty's circus employed more than 500 people. They traveled from city to city in fifteen railroad cars. The only circus larger than Beatty's at the time belonged to the Ringling Brothers.

Beatty plied his trade over a forty-year period. Interestingly enough, he never hunted animals. "I just disliked the idea of hurting or humiliating them in any way," he said.

Max Winter and Jack Dempsey had known each other since the early 1930s, when, as a young man, Winter promoted a series of exhibitions with Dempsey after he lost the heavyweight title.

I listened while Max and Jack reminisced about their youthful escapades as they toured the country during the Great Depression. Dempsey's big money days were over, and jobs were scarce. Few had extra bucks to plunk down to see Jack Dempsey fight anymore.

A decade earlier, in the roaring '20s, when Americans were enjoying great prosperity, Dempsey had been the golden boy of boxing. Fans flocked to see this one-time barroom brawler from the hobo jungles of a Western mining camp. In a world title defense against Georges Carpentier, Dempsey drew the first million-dollar gate in the history of the fight game.

Winter said, "Jack was a tiger in the ring. With his bobbing and weaving style, he was very hard to hit. Compared to today's heavyweights, he would be considered small at about 190 pounds, but he made up for it in punching power. I would say the closest to Jack's style and size was Rocky Marciano."

I asked Dempsey what he considered to be his most memorable fight.

"I would say when I won the heavyweight title from Jess Willard," the champ replied. "I'll never forget it."

That fight was held in Toledo, Ohio, on July 4, 1919.

"It was outdoors, in the afternoon, and the sun was just broiling," recalled Dempsey, reliving the events of the day. "I was almost sixty pounds lighter than he was. At 6' 6", he was much taller, too. My first few punches broke his jaw. I knocked him down seven times in the first round, and then worked him over pretty good for the next couple rounds. He was just a great big target and easy to hit. Willard couldn't come out for the fourth round. He was a mess. He had four teeth missing, his eyes were closed, his nose smashed and two ribs cracked, not to mention his broken jaw. I felt sad for him afterwards. He was a very nice man. But I had a job to do and I was thrilled to be the new heavyweight champion of the world."

Later, Dempsey became a successful New York restaurant owner. You could usually see him in the window, hosting friends and fans. He never lost his popularity.

In 1983, Jack Dempsey died of natural causes at age eighty-seven. Clyde Beatty died at age sixty-two on July 19, 1965. My dear friend Max Winter died in 1996 at the age of ninety-three.

Fast Fact: Max Winter

Under Max Winter's ownership, the Minnesota Vikings earned four Super Bowl berths (1970, '74, '75 and '77). The Vikings lost all four games.

TWENTY-FOUR

Mike Todd and Joe Resnick

Mike Todd's classic film *Around the World in 80 Days* was about to premier at the Dome, the big geodesic showroom at Henry Kaiser's Hawaiian Village Hotel in Waikiki. The local theater chains were furious and fuming that Kaiser had stepped into their territory and snatched the movie away from them. But this was the late 1950s, and what the great multi-millionaire industrialist wanted, he usually got.

A select group of media, politicos and local dignitaries from the community were invited to the screening. Lunch was held on the Dome stage after the movie. I happened to be seated across from Todd and his young wife, Elizabeth Taylor, at the long table that stretched across the Dome stage. Taylor was at the very peak of her popularity and fame. Saying she was beautiful just didn't do justice in describing her. Startling was more like it. She was drop-dead, absolutely stunningly, gorgeous. None of us, I'm sure, had ever seen such a vision of enchantment. And those incredible violet eyes! Most of the males at the long table could hardly eat. Their mouths were open, gasping at Taylor's magnificence.

Todd presented a short speech about the film, and then hung around to answer questions. He was surrounded by a phalanx of media looking for quotes. Eventually, I got close enough to the producer to ask if could interview him on my weekly TV show and also for my column.

As a self-made, fast-talking, tough New York producer, Mike Todd had more ups and downs then a hotel elevator. Rich one minute, broke the next. He also had a reputation as an inveterate gambler. He brooked no nonsense.

Mike looked at me for a moment and spat out, "Kid, don't bother me with that kind of shit. I don't have time for interviews." He quickly turned away to talk to someone else.

Disappointed, I sighed out loud, "Well, I guess I lose my bet."

Todd heard my remark, turned back to me and asked, "What bet?"

I explained that my TV sponsor, Joe Resnick, had bet me $250 I couldn't get Todd for my weekly TV show. But if I did, he'd cancel out the debt that I owed him.

"You tell that asshole sponsor of yours to forget what you owe him," Todd shot back. "You got me as your guest, pal. Tell me where you want me and what time. I'll be there."

Todd showed up and proceeded to give me one of the lousiest interviews in TV history. Apparently fancying himself a comic, he answered my questions with double talk. There was no tape in those days—everything was live—so I just went along with him while he had his little joke. Nevertheless, I won my bet. What I didn't know at that time was that Mike Todd was an avid gambler. He just couldn't pass up a challenge.

Not long after that, Todd died in a private airplane crash.

Joe Resnick is another story. He came to Hawaii from New York with five kids at the age of thirty-one. He was a very rich young man, having invented a TV antenna that made his Channel Master Corporation the leading antenna producer in the country. While in Hawaii in 1956, he decided to build pre-fab homes. That project folded a year later because of inadequate funding.

Joe was a very friendly, warm person who loved Hawaii's laid-back style. In those days, he rarely shaved or combed his hair, and he enjoyed wearing just aloha shirts, shorts and slippers and making like a beachcomber. He went everywhere like that, even to dressy functions. Many of the swankier restaurants of the day, those with a dress code, barred him from their premises. He usually smiled, shrugged and uttered a local expression, "Ain't no big thing." He didn't seem to care what people thought of him.

After three years in Hawaii, Joe returned to his upstate New York home. Soon he was back again on the road to financial success after developing other products.

It was the assassination of President Kennedy in late 1963 that lit a spark in Joe. Soon after that, he became interested in public service and politics. In fact, it started to consume him. He became a member of the school board in his area and kept broadening his political horizons. At that time, I had no communication with Joe, and I often wondered what happened to him.

Then, as I read the newspaper one day in the early '60s, my eyes popped when I saw a familiar face alongside a wire-service story about New York's newly-elected Democratic Senator from the rich Hudson Valley farm region. Joe Resnick, Congressman? My old sponsor, Joe? I almost fell over. I couldn't believe it!

In newspaper interviews, Joe credited his years in Hawaii for helping to change him. For example, "In Hawaii," he said, "I learned how people of different backgrounds can live together in harmony, if they are determined to help each other."

Joe became fairly well known nationally at the time by attacking Robert F. Kennedy, who was running for President in 1968. However, after Bobby was assassinated, Resnick was devastated. He changed his tune and declared it a great loss for the country, saying what a special man Bobby was.

In politics, Joe had finally found a career that he wanted to devote the rest of his life to. He wasn't after money anymore. Helping people—that was it. No more thoughts of just retiring. He had finally found his calling. He was never so happy.

Sadly, a year later, still in his early forties, my friend Joe Resnick died of a heart attack.

Fast Fact: Mike Todd

In high school, Mike Todd led a successful production of *The Mikado*. He later dropped out of school, however, and worked as a pharmacist, shoe salesman and store window decorator.

TWENTY-FIVE

MUHAMMAD ALI AND ANGELO DUNDEE

Muhammad Ali was in town. I quickly called his trainer, the legendary Angelo Dundee, at the Kahala Hilton and asked for an interview.

"C'mon over, and we'll have some coffee," said Angelo.

I was out of the office and on my way.

Although I was an Ali fan like millions of other boxing enthusiasts, I always wanted to meet Angelo. In the boxing world, he was definitely in a class by himself. He was an expert at training, coaching, teaching and handling his charges, molding them into the very best fighters they could be. Without question, Angelo was *the* professor of the fight game. He knew the ins and outs of the sport, yet he still kept his distance from the many unsavory characters that have always slithered in and out of the pugilistic business.

I met him at the hotel's coffee shop. Right away, Dundee sensed that I was not only a big boxing fan, but a Dundee devotee, as well. We immediately had a good rapport, and I found him to be very friendly and communicative.

Angelo first learned about the intricacies of the boxing science as a youngster hanging around the famous Stillman's Gym in New York. Born in 1921 in Philadelphia, he had dreamed of being a boxing champion himself and perhaps would have been, except for one minor obstacle: "I just didn't have the talent to be a fighter," he laughed. "So, I learned how to train those who could fight. As a result, I've enjoyed a great life working with so many champions."

The first champion he worked with was Carmen Basilio, who

held two titles: the welterweight and middleweight crowns.

When did he begin his association with Muhammad Ali?

"I had moved to Miami, opened my own gym and was doing quite well," Angelo explained. "A few years later, when Ali was signed to fight Sonny Liston for the world heavyweight championship, I was hired as Ali's trainer."

"Ali wasn't Ali then," continued Dundee. "He was still Cassius Clay, and only twenty-two years old. Also, at that time, Liston was one of the world's most feared boxers. He was a bad apple, and not many challengers wanted to tangle with him. Few people believed Ali had any chance at all. Except, of course, for Muhammad. He was totally confident. He told everybody he would knock Liston out. Of course, nobody believed him. Ali even went to Liston's training camp, and while the champ was in the ring working out, Ali was ringside, yelling at him and calling him names like 'big, ugly bear.' Ali was fearless. Boy, how the press loved this."

If you're a boxing fan, you know what happened next. February 25, 1964 in Miami Beach, Florida: Cassius Clay totally outclassed the aging Liston, forcing the champ to quit before the seventh round. Clay, in fact, was in trouble himself once in the fight, and it was because he was having a problem with his vision.

"It happened after the fourth round," Angelo told me. "Ali came back to the corner complaining that he couldn't see. We washed the eye as best we could and I told him to just stay away from Liston. Just box and dance. By the next round, his eye cleared and Ali began hitting Liston almost at will. When the bell rang for the seventh round, Liston refused to come out. He was totally defeated. He just sat exhausted on his stool, despite his handlers desperately trying to get him to fight. Ali then danced all over the ring with his hands raised over his head. He ran to where the sportswriters were, climbed the ropes and started yelling, 'I'm the greatest!' over and over."

"Was there actually something in Ali's eye?"

Although it was never proven, Dundee guessed that the cause of his fighter's temporary blindness was probably Monsel's Solution, which was used to stop Liston's cut from bleeding. In all likelihood,

Dundee said, some of it rubbed into Ali's eye during a clinch or from Liston's gloves.

Coffee and muffins were finished. It was now time to meet the man himself.

When we entered his suite, Ali was in bed, the blankets up to his chin. He had a record player next to the bed, blasting out a rock number. Angelo and I were standing at the foot of his bed when he introduced me. I walked around the bed and extended my hand.

Slowly, his hand emerged from under the covers. He shook my hand and then flipped the blankets off his body. There, in all his glory, Ali lay naked.

I couldn't resist. I had to do a show-biz shtick. I put my hands to my face, looked at his privates, and gasped like a drag queen. "Oohh, Mu-haaaa-madd!"

Ali quickly went along with the obvious gag. He grabbed his blankets, pulled them up and yelled to Dundee, 'Will you puh-leeze get this fruitcake out of here!"

We all laughed as I pranced away.

No question Ali was something special. At the time I met him, he was still in his prime—a great physical specimen, quite handsome for a fighter, with hardly a mark on his face. He was a man with a special sense of humor. Ali had more natural promotional ability than most promoters I knew.

Ali was, as they say in media circles, "good copy." He was a natural showman who gave reporters a story by being a special character. And the media ate it all up.

Today, Ali is in his early sixties. Afflicted with Parkinson's disease, his motor skills—walking and talking—are nowhere near what they once were. It could have been because of all the punishment he absorbed over his twenty-five-year boxing career.

His wife, Lonnie Ali, a lawyer who takes good care of him, says his capacity for self-expression might be diminished, but his capacity for joy is not.

I'll always remember those few special moments I once spent with him. For me and boxing fans the world over, Muhammad Ali will always be "The Greatest."

Fast Fact: Angelo Dundee

Angelo Dundee trained fifteen world champions in the sport of boxing, including Muhammad Ali, Sugar Ray Leonard and George Foreman. Dundee was also hired to train Russell Crowe for the Oscar-winning actor's role in *Cinderella Man*.

TWENTY-SIX

Otto Preminger and Burgess Meredith

Burgess Meredith was having trouble with the scene. It just wasn't being done to director Otto Preminger's satisfaction. They had shot it a number of times, and Preminger was becoming irritated. He was sweating. His face was crimson.

Finally, the famous Preminger temper flared, and he took his frustration out on poor Meredith, blasting him verbally. The scene portrayed a military press conference in a Quonset hut, and a lot of people were crowded into close quarters. It was becoming stifling and uncomfortable for everybody.

Preminger was directing *In Harm's Way*, a movie starring John Wayne and Kirk Douglas. This 1966 film was made entirely in Hawaii and was the first of a new breed of World War II movies that dealt more maturely with the disaster of Pearl Harbor. A number of real Honolulu newspaper and broadcast types were recruited to play war correspondents, and I was one of them. But I didn't get the role just like that. It took a bit of negotiation that went like this.

I "interviewed" for the part with Preminger himself at the Kahala Hilton. I was a longtime fan of Otto's. As a young man, he began his career as an actor in Europe and rose to directing in Vienna. He played a Nazi menace in a number of films, but concentrated more on directing, eventually becoming one of Hollywood's best.

"You vill enjoy da hacting experience," said the director in his thick German accent.

"Well, it depends," I said.

"Vat do you mean?" Otto wanted to know.

I explained to Preminger that many of the local news types in the movie scene were six-footers, and they would be facing John Wayne in the press conference scene. Being only 5' 7" myself, I couldn't take the chance of being put in the back of this press group. I would be totally hidden, and my opportunity for screen immortality would be lost. I was putting Preminger on, of course.

"So vat do you vant?" Otto asked, sternly. I told him I had to be in the front of the group so I could be seen.

"And if I don't okay it?" he said.

"Well, in that case, who knows what nasty things I may write about you in my column," I needled him.

He enjoyed my kidding and making my "demands." The result: Otto placed me right next to "Admiral" John Wayne in the scene. If I wanted to be noticed, however, that was no place to be standing. The man was huge! I felt like I was standing in a deep hole.

Anyway, Otto kept his word. I was actually seen. And he even gave me dialogue. (That is, if one word can be construed as dialogue.)

In the scene, Wayne says to the press that he believes America is finally moving ahead in the Pacific during the war. And I say, "Ahead?"

That was it.

When lunch was called on the set, I sat with Meredith and asked why he didn't tell Preminger off. After all, Meredith was an accomplished and distinguished actor, and Preminger had chewed him out in front of everybody.

"Oh," sighed Burgess. "Over the years, I've worked with Otto many, many times. I know him well. He didn't mean anything. Really, it was just the pressure of the job. I'm a director, too. I understand him. He's really a wonderful gentlemen and my friend."

I found Burgess to be one of the kindest and most considerate human beings I've ever met.

In 1957, after co-starring with Audie Murphy in *Joe Butterfly* in Japan, Meredith enjoyed a long-overdue vacation in Honolulu with his wife, Kaja. We had dinner one night at the Mayflower restaurant, now long gone, in Waikiki. Buck Buchwach, then the managing editor of the *Honolulu Advertiser*, joined us. We talked about many things, including Meredith's early years in the business and how he struggled to establish himself in theater and films. His father drank and quarreled constantly with his mother, and he talked about how his fine young soprano voice had helped him escape from this unhappy childhood of violence and fear. Meredith had won a series of singing competitions, and this earned him a room-and-board scholarship to the St. John Choir in New York City. He never returned to his hometown of Lakewood, Ohio.

During his college years, Burgess worked many jobs. "I was no good at anything except the stage," he admitted. Eventually, he landed a starring role in the Broadway play *Winterset*, and then he was off to Hollywood to star in the same part for the film version. From then on, Meredith enjoyed a successful career in film and on stage.

During dinner at the Mayflower, a group of husky young men sat close by and made loud comments about the strange-looking man with the unusual jet-black hair. Of course, they were talking about Burgess. He still looked a bit like the Japanese character he had just played in the *Butterfly* movie in Japan.

Finally, Meredith was fed up with the insults of the inebriated men, who were all U.S. Marines. He turned to them and politely asked them to knock it off. One of the Marines came over to our table and started insulting Meredith to his face; he even made a couple of uncalled-for cracks about Kaja. Meredith, who was about my height, stood up to the 6' 5" young man and took a swing. He missed, and the Marine retaliated. Fortunately, his knuckles just grazed Meredith's chin. Suddenly, it became a free-for-all as the other Marines came to the rescue, and other bystanders jumped in to help. It was over in seconds, thanks to the customers and staff who broke up the fracas.

As the Marines were escorted from the Mayflower, we took stock. Burgess had only a small scratch on his chin; he wasn't really hurt at all. But Buchwach, who had once been a publicist, had a glint in his eye. I could see the wheels churning. He had an idea.

It was the night before Labor Day, typically one of the slowest days of the year for news stories. "Let's have some fun," said Buck, smiling. He told us his brainstorm, and Meredith agreed to the plot.

We all went to the emergency room at Queen's Hospital so that Meredith could go on record for being treated for that chin scratch. Next, we went back to the *Advertiser*, where Buck, who then was also a stringer for the Associated Press, typed up a wire story about Meredith's "attack" in Waikiki and how Burgess bravely fought off his "assailants."

"If I'm right," said Buck, "papers on the Mainland will jump all over this story because there will be so little news to choose from."

The next morning, Meredith and his wife flew off to Los Angeles. Upon arriving, he and the missus were greeted by a throng of newsmen and TV cameras. Then he was shown a copy of the Los Angeles newspaper headline: "Burgess Meredith in Waikiki Brawl."

Fast Fact: Burgess Meredith

When Burgess Meredith portrayed the Penguin in the *Batman TV* series and movie, his "quacking" sound was really a way for him to mask his coughing. While the Penguin character smoked, Meredith had, in real life, long ago given up the habit.

TWENTY-SEVEN

Peggy Ryan

One day in 1957, a couple of years into my career as a newspaper columnist, I received a call from Ann McCormack, who gave up a successful singing career on the Mainland to marry Honolulu restaurateur Paul Livermore. (Ann had previously been married to Jackie Coogan, the child star who appeared with the legendary Charlie Chaplin.) She said she was inviting a longtime Hollywood friend to lunch.

"Would you like to interview her?" she asked.

When I heard her name, I quickly accepted.

Peggy Ryan. One of my all-time favorite screen stars!

Just hearing Peggy's name brought me back to a day when I was sixteen years old. Peggy was making a personal appearance at the TKO Theater in Boston. I brought a lunch and stayed all the way through three shows.

At that time, in the mid-1940s, Peggy and Donald O'Connor were two of the biggest stars at Universal Studios. Their musicals were gold mines. They were signed to contracts after Universal held a nationwide search for two teenagers to compete against MGM's great child stars of that era, Judy Garland and Mickey Rooney. MGM was then the biggest studio in Hollywood, not to mention the wealthiest. Their musicals were lavishly produced—mostly in color. Universal, on the other hand, was struggling. They couldn't afford color, so Peggy and Donald's productions were made in black and white. Still, they were very successful and made a lot of money for the studio.

Peggy made her first appearance in films at the age of five, after winning a dance audition in Los Angeles. At ten, she co-starred with George Murphy in a Universal film, *Top Hat*. Murphy later became a U.S. Senator.

At twelve, Peggy won an important role in the film classic *The Grapes of Wrath*, starring Henry Fonda and directed by the legendary John Ford.

At Universal, Peggy and Donald made about fifteen musicals, one right after another, that were released intermittently over the years. By the time she was twenty-one, Peggy's film career was over and she turned her attention to other show business venues—major hotels and nightclubs that offered bigger salaries than she received in films. Eventually, Peggy even appeared in a command performance for the King and Queen of England at the London Palladium.

I was quite excited. Lunch with an entertainer and film star whom I was a big fan of. This was indeed a thrill.

Peggy was as bubbly in person as she was on the screen. She was very warm and friendly. No star-like airs. During the lunch she casually asked, "So, where is Mrs. Sherman?"

"There is no Mrs. Sherman," I answered.

Her eyebrows shot upward. She paused and smiled, "Oh!"

When I learned she was staying at a Waikiki hotel near our restaurant, I asked if maybe I could walk her back. She readily agreed. She was staying at a small hotel on Beach Walk. There I met Kerry, her five-year-old daughter. Kerry was one of the sweetest, most beautiful youngsters I've ever met. Blonde and blue-eyed, she was like a little doll that had come to life. I fell in love with her instantly.

From that moment on, I saw Peggy almost every day during her stay in Hawaii. Before she left the Islands, we both professed our love. She promised she would return after she divorced her husband, Ray McDonald, who was also her dance partner.

Ray was a very talented young man, but unfortunately, he had a serious drinking problem. Whenever he got angry, he took it out on Peggy, often beating her. By the time we met, she was already planning on a divorce.

Of course, I just couldn't believe that Peggy would marry

someone like me. She was totally out of my league. Never in a million years would she return to Hawaii. I couldn't offer her anything like what she had or the life she lived.

She was a star entertainer. World famous. Played the best hotels and nightclubs. She had appeared in dozens of films from childhood and guest-starred in all the top TV shows. Me? I was just a hack newspaper columnist, way out in the blue Pacific. A great star like Peggy Ryan certainly couldn't take our Hawaii romance seriously. Marry me? Impossible.

Well, I was wrong. She got her divorce and, much to my surprise, returned to Hawaii with Kerry. A few months later, in 1958, we were married.

We honeymooned on the *Lurline*, which had been once again restored to its original luster. It was *the* luxury cruise ship of the Pacific at that time. It was also the ship that first brought me to Hawaii. How providential.

I've heard whispers that I married Peggy for her money. Nothing could have been further from the truth. Financially, Peggy was actually starting from scratch with me. Most of the money Peggy and Ray had earned was gone. A fortune went toward hospital bills and treatment for Ray's problems.

Peggy didn't seem to care. She'd already had the fame and fortune, and neither had made her really happy. She wanted a more normal, settled existence than the show biz life, and Hawaii seemed to fit the bill.

Fast Fact: Peggy Ryan

Peggy Ryan's parents performed as the vaudeville team "The Merry Dancing Ryans." Peggy joined them on stage before her second birthday.

TWENTY-EIGHT

Red Skelton

Off stage, Red Skelton almost always had an expensive cigar in his mouth or between his fingers. Ironically, he never actually smoked one. Just chewed.

Red loved Hawaii and was a frequent Island visitor for many years. One day in the early 1960s, I interviewed his wife, Gloria, on the beach at the Royal Hawaiian Hotel, where they usually stayed. I had been in her company with Red many times before and noticed she always carried a little bag with her that she seldom opened. This particular afternoon, I was curious about the contents of the bag that she guarded so zealously.

Gloria laughed, opened the bag and spilled the contents onto her beach towel. It was a small fortune in jewels. "These are my medals from Red," she explained. Then she began to describe some of their many personal battles, including the time when he was drunk and took a shot at her at home, but misfired. After each encounter, she said, Red would apologize. The apology usually included an expensive piece of jewelry.

Red Bernard Skelton practically grew up in show business. He left home at age ten to travel with a medicine show through the Midwest. At seventeen, he was married to Edna Marie Stilwell, an usher who became his vaudeville partner and later his chief writer.

The rubber-faced, carrot-topped clown had a long-running TV career, from 1951 to 1971. He also enjoyed a very successful movie life, starring in dozens of hit films. Although he could be quite risqué in private, he worked clean his entire professional life. Discussing the vulgarity that was beginning to creep into the material of many comics, he said, "Working dirty is going for the quick, cheap laugh. Some of these comedians will probably be remembered as 'old what's-his-name who mostly used dirty words.' In my day, vulgarity was taboo. I don't believe it's needed to get laughs. I haven't used that kind of material and never intend to. Neither have other comedians of my time—Bob Hope, Jack Benny and George Burns—and we did all right."

Another Red Skelton story: I was in his Royal Hawaiian suite with Jake Holk, a well-known local musician who eventually became Red's "Man Friday." Skelton was holding court for the two of us with various show biz stories about his career, while putting away one drink after another. Soon he was acting like the character in one of his most famous comedy routines, Guzzler's Gin.

I was sitting in a big easy chair. Red picked up Jake's guitar (I didn't even know he could play one), planted himself right in front of me, and began to play and sing. (I didn't know he could sing, either!) He had a beautiful, sweet voice. Most of the songs he sang were of the country variety. Song after song, for half an hour or so, I was treated to an unforgettable concert by one of America's greatest clowns. No question, it was a performance people would have paid big bucks to see.

Whenever I visited with Red during his frequent vacations in Hawaii, I asked why he never performed in the Islands. "Because I come to Hawaii to get away from all that," he said. "If I knew I had a show to do, it wouldn't be a vacation. I'd be too worried about the performance."

However, after years of requests, Red finally gave in and decided to do a one-man show at the Waikiki Shell. It was a particularly warm night, and the trade winds were on vacation. I was sitting up front in the pool area with Milton Berle and his wife, Ruth. "Uncle Miltie" was in town to begin a two-week run of the play *Last of the Red-Hot Lovers*, at Honolulu's Neal Blaisdell Center.

For an hour or so, Red had the crowd in stitches. After finishing his classic Guzzler's Gin routine, he walked off the stage to a tremendous ovation. Moments went by, and soon the crowd was becoming restless. From where Berle and I were sitting, we could look into the wings of the stage, and we saw Red sprawled out on the floor. We rushed backstage.

Berle didn't wait to find out what the problem was. It was obvious that Red couldn't go on. An audience was waiting.

He strode out onstage. "While Red is taking a little rest, I thought I'd come out and say hello," Berle said. When the audience recognized him, he was greeted with a tremendous roar. From there, Berle had everyone in the palm of his hand. Spotting a lady in a wildly colored muumuu, he asked her to stand up. She did.

"Isn't that some dress?" he marveled to the crowd. "I saw you once before at one of my shows. I never forget a dress!" The crowd erupted with laughter.

Suddenly, as if nothing had happened backstage, out walked Red. It turned out that he had fainted from the heat. He thanked Milton, and two of America's greatest comedians embraced. What a moment that was!

Side note: a couple of nights later, the Berles and the Shermans were enjoying dinner at The Third Floor restaurant at the Hawaiian Regent Hotel. At that time, Uncle Miltie was one of the best-known people in show business, affectionately known by millions as "Mr. Television."

My daughter, Kerry, was twelve years old then. She said she never heard of Milton Berle. When I told Berle this, he was startled.

"She doesn't know me?" he exclaimed, looking at her with dismay. "Well, she will."

Berle proceeded to put on a special performance just for Kerry, right there in the restaurant. He did a bunch of his show biz bits: falling off a chair, pantomime, funny faces and so on. Kerry was hysterical. She never laughed so loud in all her life!

On another of Skelton's visits, still in the 1960s, he decided to forgo Waikiki for a rented estate in Kahala. Red's sister-in-law was part of the entourage. After dinner, she and I planned to see a Japanese movie, but that particular film was sold out when we got there. Driving around looking for another movie, I spied the marquee of the old

Palace Theater on Beretania Street. In big letters, the sign spelled out, "*The Clown*—Red Skelton." Since neither one of us had seen the film, we went in and enjoyed it immensely. Red was magnificent. He was a natural for the role and turned in a very emotional performance.

On the way back to the Kahala estate, *The Clown* was all we talked about. When we got to the house, it was dark. All the lights were off. Apparently, everyone had gone to bed. As I was bidding Red's sister-in-law good night, suddenly, up popped Red from a couch in front of the fireplace, with that ever-present cigar in his hand. We excitedly told him how much we enjoyed *The Clown*.

"Never mind that," he said. "First thing you better do, Sherman, is wipe that lipstick off your fly." Of course, there was none. His sister-in-law was so furious, she turned and, without saying goodbye, stormed into her room and slammed the door behind her.

"What's she getting so angry for?" Red asked. "I was only kidding."

During a Las Vegas trip in the 1960s, I checked in with Red, who was appearing at the Sands Hotel. He invited me over to his suite. When I arrived, Red had a palette in one hand and a paintbrush in the other. And, of course, he had an unlit cigar in his mouth. That was the first I knew about Red's passion for painting clowns.

There was a long period when Red's clown art was in big demand in Waikiki. Center Art Gallery, a prominent high-end art store on Kalakaua Avenue, sold millions of dollars' worth of his originals for many years. Some of his paintings went for as much as $100,000. The establishment eventually closed when the gallery's owners were indicted for some art hanky panky and sent to jail.

The greatest tragedy in Red's life was losing his twelve-year-old son, Richard, who was stricken with leukemia. When he learned the boy was dying, Red was devastated. He kept the news from Richard and did his best to make his last days happy ones. He even took him around the world. They spent a lot time in Hawaii, a place that Richard loved so much.

The British press printed a cruel story that claimed Red was using Richard's illness for publicity. Reportedly, Richard read the story and learned that he was dying.

Richard died on May 11, 1958, his birthday. It's said that he died while holding a crucifix that was blessed by the Pope himself.

Picasso once said that he had spent his entire life trying to recapture the innocence and sensitivity of a child.

Red Skelton never lost those qualities.

Fast Fact: Red Skelton

Red Skelton was deeply hurt by CBS' decision to cancel his TV show in 1970. In 1986, after receiving a standing ovation at the Emmy Awards show, he remarked, "I want to thank you for sitting down. I thought you were pulling a CBS and walking out on me."

TWENTY-NINE

Richard Boone

Richard Boone was one of the most complex stars I've had the pleasure of knowing. He was tall (6' 2") and husky, with a little potbelly, when I met him in the 1960s. By the time he decided to settle in Hawaii, Boone had achieved a successful and distinguished film and TV career. American TV critics thrice named him "Best Actor." He was also selected "Best Actor Starring in a Regular Series" for the show *Medic* and "Best Actor (Leading Role) in a Dramatic Series" for *Have Gun—Will Travel*.

In the mid-1940s, Boone joined the famous Actor's Studio in New York, where his classmates included such then-unknowns as Marlon Brando and Karl Malden. Before returning to California a few years later, he had appeared in some 150 live TV shows. His big break came when he snagged the lead in *Have Gun—Will Travel*, which ran from 1957 to 1961.

Boone played the role of Paladin, a San Francisco gentleman-adventurer who hires himself out as a mercenary gunslinger in the years after the Civil War. Paladin was a completely unique Western character, and the show was a fixture in the top-ten TV ratings for years.

However, like Jack Lord after *Hawaii Five-O* producer Leonard Freeman died, Boone's popularity with the *Have Gun* cast and CBS TV executives plummeted significantly. The reason: Boone became very difficult to work with. He practically took over the production. He had his hand in everything: scripts, actors, directors and even costumes. Everything had to have his personal approval.

The motivating factor that brought Boone to Hawaii, it seemed, was to enroll his son, Peter, at Punahou, one of the top private schools in the country. Boone was basically an intellectual who liked to hide behind the image of the tough, hardened cowboy actor. No question, he was usually a no-nonsense, rugged type of guy. He was also a heavy smoker and drinker.

I remember how he delighted in telling me (quite a few times, I might add) about a scene he'd done in a Western with an actress he considered a bit snobbish. He decided to teach her a lesson. The scene called for Boone to grab this woman and push her to the ground. It was quite simple to choreograph the action. However, when the director cried "Action!" Boone grabbed her, all right—by a breast. She screamed, for real, as he flung her to the ground. Of course, he feigned innocence, saying he was only trying to be realistic.

Through a number of interviews I did with him, we became friendly enough that I received frequent invitations to his Diamond Head home. During one of those sessions, I told him about a story I'd written for a possible TV project of the movie-of-the-week variety. It was about a down-on-his-luck sea captain living on a small boat at the Ala Wai Yacht Harbor. One day, there's a fire on a nearby boat. The grizzled sea captain rescues a little girl, but her parents perish in the blaze. So he raises her.

After he read the story, he thought might be something for him to do. So, we began working on the project.

Several times a week for a period of months, we'd meet at his house. Eventually, to my chagrin, the meetings became fewer and fewer and eventually dwindled down to zero. Actually, nothing much was accomplished regarding the script. The story practically remained as I had first written it.

One day much later, in 1968, it was announced that Boone was to star in a movie called *Kona Coast*, to be filmed on the Big Island. A friend of mine who was working on the project managed to get a copy of the script and sent it to me. It was about a down-on-his-luck sea captain who rescues a little girl from a fire on a nearby boat. Her parents die, and the sea captain adopts the girl and raises her.

I felt like I'd been crapped on. I felt betrayed, double-crossed.

A lawyer friend told me to forget about it. It wasn't worth fighting over; besides, it's not like I had the money for a lengthy court battle.

My revenge? The film turned out to be a disaster—el floppo—and was quickly forgotten.

From 1964 through 1971, Boone enjoyed a very comfortable life with his wife and son, who did complete his schooling at Punahou. Occasionally, Boone ventured back to the Mainland to make movies, including *Hombre* in 1966 and *The Kremlin Letter* in 1969.

Boone once intimated that he was offered the Steve McGarrett role in *Hawaii Five-O*, but declined. However, I never heard Lenny Freeman, the show's producer, ever mention such thing. The only actor I know of who was ever offered the McGarrett role other than Jack Lord was Lloyd Bridges, when Freeman planned on firing Lord.

Probably to keep from being bored, Boone decided to run for political office. So he threw his hat into the ring for lieutenant governor in the early 1960s. The announcement caused a brief stir in Hawaii and then quickly faded.

When Boone returned to the Mainland, he kept busy with the TV series *Hec Ramsey*, which ran for a couple of years in the early 1970s. He also filmed a number of made-for-TV movies and did the lecture circuit at various colleges around the country.

Boone passed away in 1981 at the age of sixty-three. He was buried in Hawaii.

Fast Fact: Richard Boone

Richard Boone's last movie role was in the 1981 film *The Bushido Blade*. Boone played Commodore Matthew Perry. Toshiro Mifune, James Earl Jones and Sonny Chiba were also in the movie.

THIRTY

SAMMY AMALU

In the early 1960s, a banner *Honolulu Advertiser* headline shocked Hawaii out of its Polynesian paralysis. The Sheraton hotel chain was offered millions for its Waikiki properties by a Swiss group. This same mysterious group was also offering millions more for whole slew of other quality Sheraton properties in Hawaii. Nobody knew who the potential buyers were, and rumors were flying all over the place.

I happened to be walking through the Royal Hawaiian Hotel for a luncheon date when I bumped into Richard Boonisar, one of Sheraton's top executives, who lived in Boston.

"I'm here to check out this so-called offer for our hotels," Richard told me. "Frankly, I think it's all a bunch of bull. We can't even locate the people who are supposedly making the offer."

Richard turned out to be right. In time, the truth surfaced: the deal was 100-percent phony. And the scam was concocted by the greatest con man Hawaii ever produced. His name was Sammy Amalu.

Now, you may be wondering, "Who's Sammy Amalu? And why does this man have his own chapter in a book about celebrities—greats like Sinatra, Elvis and Brando?"

Well, Sammy may not have been a famous celebrity in national circles, but in Hawaii he was a fairly well-known character. (And I do mean *character*!) He was a huckster, a con man—and he was damn good at what he did. Chances are, he would have carved out an even bigger reputation for himself if he'd had the opportunity.

If only he weren't in jail so much.

After days of headlines and rumors of all kinds, Sammy's name finally surfaced: Samuel Crowningburg Amalu, son of famed beach boy Charles Amalu, was possibly behind the whole scheme. This was the same charismatic Sammy, glib of tongue with an incredible knowledge of Hawaiiana (much of it created in his own mind), and writer of bum checks for non-existent banks that continually landed him in prison.

The story goes that Sammy had just gotten out of the can for the umpteenth time. Upon returning to Honolulu and while driving into town, he picked up a couple young hitchhikers who looked like surfers, and brought them back to his hotel. There, he hatched his Swiss hui (business group) charade. He made his new friends his "pro regents," or royal couriers, who made the hotel offers.

It was said Sammy would never hurt a fly unless it was attached to a sailor's pants. He loved to create hoaxes. He regarded fact and fiction as interchangeable. He loved attention. He had a lighthearted air about him and just enjoyed creating commotion. He seemed to live in his own fantasy world.

He never meant to hurt anyone. Sammy was just—well, he was Sammy.

Shortly after his Sheraton hoax, he passed another of his useless checks and was subsequently jailed in San Francisco. I flew there with a TV camera crew for my first interview with Sammy. When he entered the office that was provided for the interview, I was surprised at his appearance: medium height and build, totally bald and with teeth that looked decayed. When we greeted each other, he offered a limp hand, dangling his fingers.

Speaking with a cultured English accent, Sammy was absolutely charming. He was obviously very astute about life in prison. I asked him what job he had. He replied that the two best jobs in any jail are being the chaplain's assistant and being in charge of the library.

"And what's your job?" I asked.

He smiled, "Both of them."

In the middle of the interview, there was a knock on the door, so we stopped filming. A prisoner stuck his head in and handed Amalu two packs of cigarettes. "Thank you," he said. "You may be dismissed, my good man." Then he waved the prisoner off as though he were the president of a major organization.

As *Advertiser* editor George Chaplin noted, Sammy's thirst for check kiting remained unquenchable. A month after his release from jail, Sammy wrote two rubber checks on the same day—May 22, 1963. One was for $26,000 for a Cadillac, and the other for $73,000 for seven British-made automobiles. Naturally, this resulted in yet another prison sentence.

Back in the can, he hoodwinked a prison cook into trying to cash $200,000 in checks at a local bank. This got him transferred to Folsom, a high-security prison. Because he needed an outlet for his creative expression, he started sending graphic letters about Hawaiian history to the *Advertiser*'s publisher, Thurston Twigg-Smith. Thus, he became America's only federal prison columnist writing for a metropolitan newspaper.

Eventually, when Sammy was released from prison, he signed on with the paper as a featured columnist. There were those who claimed that the Hawaiian history that Amalu wrote was pure fiction. Nevertheless, he gained a large following and reveled in his work.

When he walked through the *Advertiser* city room, most reporters ignored him. I, on the other hand, happily welcomed him, and Sammy and I often chatted for long periods of time in my office. He was a kick. I appreciated his strange but unique showmanship. Whether his stories were true or false, the way he told them was absolutely fantastic. He was a real literary talent. He had a great gift for words.

Sammy was just a one-of-a-kind character. He made you believe he was for real. You *wanted* to believe that he was for real. But, in reality, he lived in his own fantasyland. I never knew another person like him. Sammy was an absolute original who would have made a great actor had he chosen that profession. He died in 1986 at age sixty-eight.

Many years before his death, Sammy wrote his own obituary. Here are just a few lines:

"Sing no sad songs over my mortal dust. Tell me no gentle lies to wash more chaste the wanton waste of my days...I have known laughter. I have known tears. I have tasted victory. I have sipped of failure. Is not all this enough?...'He was a child of princes, and the dust of his flesh was fashioned of Hawaii's soil.' Say only this of me and no more."

Fast Fact: Sammy Amalu

Sammy Amalu was a Punahou School classmate of Thurston Twigg-Smith, publisher of the *Honolulu Advertiser*. Amalu's column in the *Advertiser* ran until 1984.

THIRTY-ONE

SAMMY DAVIS, JR.

I first met Sammy Davis, Jr., in 1953. We met in Montreal, during my stand-up comedy career. He was appearing with his father and uncle at the Chez Paree, the city's number-one nightclub. At the time, I was employed at the Top Hat, a small club on St. Catherine Street.

After my show one evening, I dropped into a club where a comic pal from Boston, Lou Daley, was appearing. When I arrived, Lou was hosting a small group of friends before the show.

I walked over, shook Lou's hand and wished him luck. He said thanks and, to my surprise, basically brushed me off. He didn't ask me to join his friends at their table.

I just shrugged, turned around and started to walk away. Suddenly, somebody grabbed my arm. It was very dim in the club, and I couldn't make out the face.

"You in show biz?" a voice asked.

"Yes, over at the Top Hat," I answered. "I just came by to wish Lou luck."

The voice said, "Then join us, man. Have a seat."

I still couldn't recognize the man's face. He then popped a cigarette in his mouth and lit it.

It was Sammy Davis, Jr.

After the show, Sammy invited me to his hotel the next day. When I arrived, he greeted me at the door only wearing his white boxer shorts. He had a gold chain around his neck with a mezuzzah hanging from it. A large diamond was right in its center.

I said, "How come you're wearing a mezuzzah?"

His face lit up. "Eddie Cantor gave it to me after I did his television show—the Colgate Comedy Hour," he said. "And I wear it proudly because I also happen to be Jewish."

That was a surprise.

For the next two weeks, Sammy and I were almost inseparable. We roamed Montreal together by day—seeing the sights, having dinner, going to movies. Just hanging out. A non-stop talker, Sammy told me stories about his life in show business—the people he'd met, his experiences, his dreams.

He was on stage, he told me, from the time he could walk. The Wil Mastin Trio (which consisted of Sammy, his dad and his uncle Wil) played what seemed like every city, town, hamlet and backwater in America. They stayed in third-rate hotels and suffered the bigotry and racial discrimination of the times.

Swapping tales of some of the worst dives we ever worked in, I told Sammy about a joint in Lynn, Massachusetts, where the entertainers dressed in a coal bin in the cellar of the club. To get to the so-called showroom, we had to walk up the cellar stairs and climb through a trap door that led us to the club's kitchen.

Sammy threw his head back and laughed. "The Tic Tock Club! Yeah, man, in Lynn, Massachusetts! We also played that toilet. I think the Trio made about $25 for the week."

Sammy had practically no formal schooling, which meant show business was his life. He lived and breathed the business. It was all he knew.

"The trouble with so many performers, especially some who have made it to the top, is that they don't always come up with the best that's in them when they're on stage," he said, sharing his philosophy about entertainers. "There's really no excuse for that. When I go to see and hear a performer who is supposed to be great, I expect the best."

The years passed. Sammy's star ascended to the stratosphere. Many people began referring to him as the greatest entertainer of his time. It was hard to disagree.

We finally met again in the early 1960s. It was in Honolulu, where he was scheduled for a concert. He arrived via Australia, where he had shattered box office records in Sydney and Melbourne. I went out to the airport to welcome him.

After I greeted him with a lei, he told me he only had a couple of hours before his next flight. So I invited him to my house to relax and clean up.

"Cool, daddy," he replied. "But first I wanna buy some Hawaiian shirts and a few muumuus for my family."

At the airport gift shop, he quickly selected the merchandise, tossed a few hundred-dollar bills on the counter, and said he'd pick it all up in a few hours.

"Keep the change," he said, flashing that now-familiar smile.

When we got to my house, I pointed to a rainbow in the sky. "That's good for postcards, but what do you do for laughs?" he asked. Show biz talk.

Even when relaxed, Davis was like a ticking bomb. His outbursts on a variety of subjects were almost as dynamic as his performances.

"That Australia flipped me out," he told me. "I went there with very little going for me. They hadn't seen me on TV or in movies, and I don't think they knew too much about my records. The first night we had a small crowd, but the promoters papered the house (gave away free tickets). Then the first-night folks spread the word and the reviews, believe me, were the best I've ever had in my life!

"That Australian press was just a gas. Too much. After that we had sellout crowds of 10,000 for twice a night. They went for everything, even the hip stuff. What an experience!"

Fast-forward to 1964. Sammy and I were sitting around the Kahala Hilton pool one day during a two-week vacation he was enjoying in Hawaii. When he jumped up and started to slather suntan lotion all over his body, I couldn't resist asking, "Sammy, you already have a tan. What's with the lotion?"

"Hey, schmuck," he laughed. "I may be black, but we sho' do burn, too, just like you white guys."

At that time, Sammy had just published his autobiography, *Yes I*

Can. I went to a bookstore, bought a copy of the 612-page book and devoured it. I was left with a large lump in my throat from the dramatic and emotional heart tugs strewn throughout his story.

Besides detailing his climb to the dizzying heights of show business, Sammy's autobiography detailed unbelievable instances of inhumanity against a small man, not particularly attractive, who was born with dark skin and gifted with one of the most extraordinary talents ever exhibited in the entertainment world.

This dynamic, brave man reached out with his tremendous abilities, in the spotlight of the profession he was born into, with the heart of a lion. He overcame beatings, insults, humiliation and hatred. He was spat upon and suffered indignities that would have made a lesser individual pack his dreams in mothballs.

What drove Sammy? "I had to be a star like another man has to breathe," he wrote in *Yes I Can*. "I had to get bigger. I wanted to get so big, so powerful, so famous that the day would come when they'd look at me and see a man and then somewhere along the way they'll notice he just happens to be black."

The last time I saw Sammy was in March 1989, at a concert in Honolulu's Neal Blaisdell Arena with Liza Minnelli and Frank Sinatra. Frank and Sammy were in the twilight of their careers. But talent does not age. They were three of the greatest entertainers in my lifetime.

Fast Fact: Sammy Davis, Jr.

Sammy Davis, Jr., was one of the first male celebrities to admit to being a fan of TV soap operas. This eventually led Davis to a recurring role as Chip Warren in *One Life to Live*. The role landed him a Daytime Emmy nomination in 1980.

THIRTY-TWO

Sophia Loren

It was spring of 1972, and I was in Rome, sitting with one of the most beautiful and talented ladies in the entire film world. Her name?

Sophia Loren.

At the time, Loren was in the midst of filming *Man of La Mancha*, co-starring Peter O'Toole. Budgeted at $11 million, the film had a six-month shooting schedule.

As I watched a scene being filmed, Loren, somewhat begrimed and showing a nice bit of leg through her peasant garb, hardly looked like the reigning queen of Italian cinema. Her hair was daubed with mud and styled with a medieval version of the frizzies and was only slightly cleaner than the matted locks of the other thirty-odd inmates of the dungeon, where she'd spent the past few weeks portraying the sullen-eyed Aldonza.

This was a physically demanding role for Loren. She'd been taunted, tormented and manhandled by a rough group of mule drivers who, even in play-acting, left her bruised and sore.

At the end of her shooting day, after a quick shower and a change into jeans and a blouse, Loren again looked like the glamorous lady who, after twenty years on the screen, was considered Europe's only remaining superstar.

I had to wait about an hour for the interview. The reason for the delay? She had been deep into Pistol, one of the card games she played daily with co-stars O'Toole and James Coco.

"I'm so sorry," she told me, "but I was ahead $500…"

The image of a stunning woman like Sophia Loren beating men

at poker and taking their money made me laugh.

Why, I asked Sophia, did she want to take on a frowzy and physically demanding role like Aldonza at this stage of her career?

"I've always wanted to do a musical, and this is the first such role I could believably play," she replied. "I understand the character of Aldonza. She had to fight for everything in her life, every crust of bread. I know that from my own childhood."

And yes, Loren did her own singing in the movie. "I worked for nearly two months to learn the four numbers I sing," she told me. "I don't think I have to be ashamed of my vocal performance."

Then thirty-seven, Loren had everything a film legend's career had to offer. She and her husband, producer Carlo Ponti, lived in a seventeen-room villa fourteen miles from Rome. Her greatest love was her three-year-old son, Carlo Jr. She had already enrolled him at Eton in England.

The other highlight of my trip to Rome was visiting the Vatican and having an audience with the Pope. It was Holy Week, and Rome was jam-packed. Everyone gathered in Audience Hall, which had been dedicated the previous year.

Over 12,000 holders of hard-to-get-tickets—many people waited for hours to get them—leaped to their feet as one when Pope Paul VI entered from the back of the hall, carried in on a throne. People screamed "Papa! Papa!" as flashbulbs created a pyrotechnic atmosphere. As the Pope moved down the aisle, babies were thrust at him and hundreds of hands reached out to touch the Holy Father. He smiled at everyone, blessing all.

Before going into Audience Hall, my wife, Peggy, purchased a handful of religious medals. When the Pope gave his blessings, we were told that they also touched the families of people in attendance, plus religious mementos they had with them. In all, the audience lasted an hour. What a memorable experience!

Fast Fact: Sophia Loren

Sophia Loren's sister, Anna Maria Scicolone, was formerly married to the son of dictator Benito Mussolini.

THIRTY-THREE

SUGAR RAY ROBINSON

Sugar Ray Robinson was called "pound-for-pound the greatest fighter of all time." I was among the many millions of fight fans who believed this. From the time I was a kid Sugar Ray was my idol.

In the summer of 1965, in the twilight of his incredible career, Robinson came to Honolulu to fight Stan Harrington. Young, aggressive and ambitious, Harrington was then Hawaii's middleweight champion.

The first time I met Robinson, the five-time world champion was carrying a Bible. "I read the Good Book every chance I get," he told me. "Not long ago, I bought a building in the Bronx, which is now the Holy Light Baptist Church. I did this for my mother, who is very active in the church as the minister's secretary."

Even though he was way beyond his prime—he was now an old man in the fight game—Sugar Ray was hoping for one more chance at the middleweight crown. "If I'm successful, I shall quit boxing for good," he said.

"What will you do then?" I asked him.

He smiled. "I've always loved show business. When I retired a few years ago, briefly, I played nightclubs. I'm not too bad as a singer and dancer," he laughed. "In a few months, I'll be taking over the Sammy Davis role in *Golden Boy*." Much of that Broadway musical hit had been based on Sugar Ray's life.

"Sammy came to me and asked if I'd be interested," he explained, "since he wanted a few months off from the show. Not many people know this, but I've been studying voice at the suggestion of Richard

Rogers, who wrote the show's music. He got me a singing teacher, and I work with him every day I'm in New York. Mr. Rogers believes I have talent and has been most encouraging. I study singing with the same determination I've given to boxing. I also play drums and dance. God has been good to me."

For most of his one-week stay in Honolulu, Ray relaxed and did some light workouts. I got a better insight into his character while dining with him over a plate of smoked ribs at the old Kalia Garden. Also with us was Ray's girlfriend and future wife, Ruby.

A philosophical, soft-spoken man, Ray noted, "Most people are lucky if they get one chance up at bat in life. I've had many, thanks to the good Lord. I've had fame and riches, but I've learned it's more important to be a good human being. Man's greatest battle is to earn the respect of his fellow man. That has to be won. Nobody just gives it to you. No matter how well known you are, or how big your bank account is, there is no guarantee you'll have respect, too."

His face was smooth, with no visible souvenirs from his many battles, save for some hardly noticeable scar tissue over his left eye.

"Many of my friends ask me why I keep fighting; they say I should quit before I get hurt," he continued, shaking his head. "I'm forty-four, but I don't believe an athlete's chronological age tells the true story. I've never smoked or drank or done drugs. I always kept myself in the best condition, never abusing my body."

August 10, 1965. Fight night. Honolulu's old Civic Auditorium was packed.

The first round was a gem. Sugar Ray looked he like was in his prime for the first three minutes. He danced like the master he once was, jabbing, hooking and tying up Harrington at will. He was Sugar Ray, the champ.

Sadly, that was it.

After that, Ray ran out of gas. For the next nine rounds, Harrington swarmed all over him. A hard left hook connected to Robinson's eye, and the blood spurted for the rest of the fight. His corner men couldn't stop the flow. Sugar Ray was strictly on the defensive for the rest of the battle, exhibiting a masterly display of boxing and doing his best to hold on while youth triumphed. Harrington easily won a ten-round decision against the legend. The crowd loved the battle, however, and gave Robinson an ovation for his effort.

Only a few people, including his handlers and Ruby, were in Ray's dressing room after the fight. The legend was sitting disconsolately as his gloves were being removed. I congratulated him on a fine show, shook his hand and started to leave. "Don't go," he said. "Can you meet me at the hotel?"

I wound up spending three hours with Sugar Ray and Ruby in the hotel room after the fight. Ray was spent. Exhausted. He stretched out on his bed and just talked and talked, as though he were unburdening himself to a psychiatrist.

One of the stories he told us that night was about a fight he once had when he was drugged, but didn't know it. As the fight progressed, he recalled, his arms became progressively heavier. By the end of the fight, he could hardly lift his arms! Yet, somehow, he miraculously won. Ray eventually found out what happened. His handlers—his own people—had got great odds on the fight and bet against Ray. To insure their bet, they drugged him.

"And, believe it or not, some of the guys are still with me," he said. "I forgave them. They needed money. They tried to beat me. But they lost. That's life. No need to hold grudges."

Fast Fact: Sugar Ray Robinson

In 2006, Sugar Ray Robinson became only the second boxer to have his likeness printed on a U.S. postage stamp. The other fighter to receive this honor was Joe Louis.

THIRTY-FOUR

Tommy Sands

Tommy Sands was one of America's early rock idols. He was young, handsome, talented and right on the threshold of a huge show business career. He even had Colonel Tom Parker as a manager. Recording contracts, sellout personal appearances, movie stardom—Tommy had it all.

And then, like a puff of smoke, it all seemed to vanish overnight.

I first met Tommy in 1958, when he was still a teenager. He was the headline act at the Civic Auditorium. The previous year had been a breakthrough year for Tommy. His first film, *The Singing Idol*, was a smash hit. He followed by starring in a TV movie, also titled *The Singing Idol*. And from that came his biggest hit, "Teen-Age Crush." Suddenly, Tommy Sands was a hot commodity; he was one of America's brightest young stars.

Still, trouble was on the horizon. Parker had just signed another youngster who was making waves. Some kid named Elvis. It was inevitable that comparisons were drawn between the two. Eventually, of course, Parker concentrated all his efforts on Elvis. Tommy was cast adrift.

I noted in my newspaper review of his Civic performance that Tommy displayed a talent that would keep him in demand for many years to come. And, that unlike so many of that era, namely Elvis Presley, Tommy sang with hardly any hip swinging. I said it was a decided asset to his well-rounded, clean-cut display. (Admittedly, I was certainly wrong about the hip swinging!)

Years went by. One day in 1968, I heard a rumor that Tommy had quietly returned to Hawaii—not as a tourist, but as a patient at the state mental hospital in Kaneohe. I checked. It was true. He had voluntarily checked himself in.

I went to visit him at my first opportunity. When he was ushered into the waiting room, I almost didn't recognize this famous young man who, just a few years earlier, had been one of America's biggest entertainment stars. He was dressed in the hospital's white gown. He had a beard and long, shaggy hair.

What happened? My head buzzed at the seemingly tragic situation. How could he tumble into oblivion like this? Was it the loss of his career? Was it his divorce from his wife, Nancy Sinatra?

What happened?

His psychiatrist answered some of the questions. Tommy just couldn't handle everything that was happening in his life. He needed strength to face reality. Enter drugs. They had the usual damaging effect. It almost destroyed Tommy. The doctor said that Tommy had almost totally lost his self-esteem and confidence to face the world. In a nutshell, he just couldn't handle living anymore.

Tommy seemed to appreciate my visit and asked me to return. And I did, usually with my wife. We'd take Tommy out to dinner almost every weekend. I told his friend, promoter Tom Moffatt, about the situation, and soon he also started visiting Tommy.

Eventually, Moffatt and I started discussing the inevitable: a possible comeback for Sands. His doctor thought it could be in the cards, but not right away. He needed more shoring up. Eventually, the doctor gave the green light. Tommy seemed to have gained more confidence as the months went by. Moffatt and I started looking for a showroom venue in Waikiki. At that time, there was just nothing available. This was in the 1960s, when Waikiki was red-hot. All the top entertainment rooms were in use.

One day, when we explained our Tommy problem to Mike Hickey, then general manager of the Outrigger Waikiki Hotel, he said, "We just don't have anything at the moment, but I have an idea. Let me work on it."

A few weeks later, we had another meeting with Hickey. "I've convinced the hotel to take a chance with Tommy Sands," he told us.

"We have a large storage area just off the lobby that we'll clean out and convert into a showroom. It would be the perfect location."

Hickey was true to his word. Within months, the storage area was transformed into a beautiful, first-class showroom. And Tommy Sands was the first star to play there. From day one, business was solid. Sands appeared as though he didn't have a problem in the world. His voice was strong, and he was giving excellent performances. Crowds came in droves.

Although she was divorced from Tommy, Nancy Sinatra called me to ask about him whenever she visited Honolulu with her husband, choreographer Hugh Lambert, and their children. She was happy to hear the good news about the show. She even asked to see him, but Tommy always refused. It wasn't because he didn't like Nancy. He didn't want to see her because he felt he couldn't handle the situation emotionally. Nancy understood. However, she did come to see his show and was very proud of his success in Hawaii.

There were rumors and magazine articles at the time hinting that Tommy was "hiding" in Hawaii because he couldn't get work on the Mainland. He was being blacklisted, the story goes, because his former father-in-law was unhappy about his split from Nancy and turned "thumbs down" on him. Nothing could have been further from the truth. Frank Sinatra did not interfere in Tommy's career. Nor did he try to hurt him professionally. And Tommy never once said an unkind word about Frank. Rather, he always spoke about Frank with the greatest admiration and respect.

For a year or so, things went smoothly. Crowds kept flocking to the Outrigger's showroom. The hotel was happy. They had a winner. Tommy Sands was back in action and was getting ready to step into the main arena of show biz again.

And, then, out of the blue, it happened.

One night, Tommy bounced on stage for his first number. As usual, Moffatt and I stood next to the spotlight in the back of the showroom. As Tommy started to sing, it was quickly evident to us that the orchestra was playing one song while Tommy was singing a totally different tune. The audience was puzzled, but thought it was part of the show. What the hell was going on?

We knew immediately. Tommy was in another world. He was flying on something.

As soon as the number was finished, the lights blacked out. Moffatt and I rushed to the stage, grabbed Sands and dragged him back to the dressing room. Sands fought with us, claiming he was fine. But we kept him in the dressing room. For Tommy, it was over. That was the end of his comeback.

Eventually, Tommy settled in Hawaii permanently and became a businessman. More importantly, he seemed to put his demons to rest. He married, had children and became a solid citizen.

Today, there's a great interest in rock stars of the 1960s, and Tommy is on the comeback circuit once again, playing various venues all around the world.

Fast Fact: Tommy Sands

Tommy Sands starred with Annette Funicello in the 1960 remake of *Babes in Toyland*.

THIRTY-FIVE

Walter Dornberger

I have been a teetotaler all my life, so sitting around a bar is not something you'd usually find me doing. However, one day in the early 1960s, I was at the Royal Hawaiian Hotel in Waikiki, killing some time before my next meeting. I took a seat at the open-air Mai Tai Bar along the beach wall, and ordered a Tab.

Soon, a short, stocky, aging bald man sat down next to me. We exchanged pleasantries. The man had a thick German accent. After the line of questioning familiar to many a tourist—"Where are you from?" "How are you enjoying Hawaii?"—I asked the gentleman what he did for a living. He told me he was a key consultant for Bell Aircraft Corporation.

I asked his name.

"Walter," he replied.

He told me he was originally from Germany and, upon arriving in America, had worked for the U.S. Air Force for a few years. Being the curious type, I asked him what his specialty was.

"Guided missiles," he said.

He seemed to enjoy the mai tais he was consuming. He had quite a few. I don't think he realized the drinks' potency, because soon his tongue loosened, and he babbled on and on about his past life in Germany.

Walter eventually told me that he'd invented the German V-2 rocket. I just smiled.

"Of course you did," I said, humoring him. *Uh-oh*, I thought, *where did this nut escape from?*

I recalled reading about Werner von Braun, the great German

rocket scientist who was one of Germany's key developers of rocket weapons. I asked Walter if he knew Von Braun.

His response was a raucous laugh.

"My dear man," he said, "Werner was my protégé. I was the director of Germany's rocket and missile programs. I met von Braun when he was nineteen years old. He was a brilliant student. We worked together on Germany's most powerful rockets."

I wasn't exactly convinced. *I might as well humor this guy and let him ramble*, I thought to myself.

"Early in the war, I went to Hitler," he continued, "and asked him to make our rocket program the number-one priority. He refused. That's why we lost the war."

"You mean you *knew* Hitler? You actually talked to him?"

"But of course," he answered. "Two years later, he came to me and told me he was making the V-2 rocket program his number-one priority. I told him it was too late. The war was lost."

"So how did you get to America?" I wanted to know.

"I eventually surrendered to the U.S. Army and the Russians," he said. "I spent two years in prison. It's a long story. After my release, I was allowed to come to America."

When I returned to the *Advertiser* later that afternoon, I went to editor George Chaplin's office and told him about this goofball character that I had met at the Royal. "He claimed to be the father of German rocketry," I laughed.

George reached for a book from his jam-packed library and handed it to me.

"I think you'll find your friend's name in there," he said.

I couldn't believe what I read. The man I'd talked to that afternoon was indeed Walter Dornberger, *the* father of Germany rocketry. The book had his picture and the whole story. He was for real. What he told me was no fantasy; it was all true!

I had met the man who nearly helped Germany win World War II.

Back in the 1930s, Dornberger was in charge of the solid-fuel rocket research program for the German Army. He met von Braun when he was only a teenager shooting off homemade rockets in his backyard. Together, they developed their first rocket a few years later. During the war, they and a team of scientists designed and constructed their new secret weapon: the V-2. It carried a single-ton warhead capable of supersonic speed—and could fly at an altitude of fifty miles. This was the famed rocket that almost wiped out London and devastated Great Britain.

Dornberger told me that he and Braun were captured at the war's end, along with all the other German scientists.

"The Russians and Americans split us up," he said. "We had about forty scientists on our project. The Russians let our people continue from where they were on the projects. Not the Americans. They scrapped everything. We had to start all over again."

That was the reason, he explained, that America fell behind the Russians in the space program at that time.

When I called the hotel later that day, hoping for a more in-depth interview with my friend at the bar, it was too late. Dornberger had already checked out.

Fast Fact: Walter Dornberger

Upon surrendering to the U.S. Army in the final days of World War II, Walter Dornberger said that he never intended for his V-2 rockets to be directed at civilian targets.

THIRTY-SIX

WALTER WINCHELL

Early on in my career as a *Honolulu Advertiser* columnist, I received a letter from Herb Caen, the most popular columnist on the West Coast. Caen claimed that I had "borrowed" a phrase he created, "Whee The People." He said that he'd invented these words about thirty years previously, and asked if I would please cease and desist from using them.

I wrote Caen back, saying, in effect, "Sorry, but I had never read your column because I lived most of my early life on the East Coast, although I had heard about you and had read your column a few times since moving to Honolulu."

As for Caen's accusation that I swiped his phrase, he was simply wrong.

When I was ten years old, I sold newspapers at Harvard Square in Boston, at the subway entrance near that great institution, Harvard University. At that time, newspapers cost two cents, and I got to keep half of that. On a good night, if I could sell a hundred papers (which seldom happened), I'd make a whole dollar!

Nevertheless, it was during this time that I began my longtime newspaper-reading habit.

I fell in love with a columnist named Walter Winchell. He was so exciting to read, even if, I must admit, I didn't always understand his columns. Most times, I had no clue about the people he wrote about.

Still, I became a big fan of the man. I read his column at every opportunity and listened faithfully to his weekly radio broadcast. He had a magical way with words. As Neal Gabler wrote in his biography of Winchell: "He wrote his column in an original smart, slangy style, inventing words and phrases. Couples didn't get married in Winchell's column; they were welded. They didn't have fun; they 'made whoopee!' They didn't have babies. They had 'blessed events.'

"Winchell introduced a revolutionary column that reported who was romancing whom, who was cavorting with the gangsters, who was ill or dying, who was suffering financial difficulties, which spouses were having affairs, which couples were about to divorce, and dozens of other secrets, peccadilloes and imbroglios that had been concealed from public view."

In other words, Winchell invented the modern gossip column. If there had been no Walter Winchell, there would never have been an Eddie Sherman.

His radio shows began with a telegraph ticker clicking. Then his high-pitched voice would blast out, "Good evening, Mr. and Mrs. North and South America and all the ships at sea. Let's go to press!" while the ticker continued in the background, much like the ticking clock on *60 Minutes*. For early radio, it was all very dramatic and riveting—and what showmanship!

By one estimate, fifty million Americans either listened to his weekly broadcast or read his daily column. Once, when he switched papers in New York, an estimated 200,000 readers followed him. According to one report, nearly half the readership of the famous Hearst newspaper chain could be attributed to Winchell's column. His audience, noted one observer, was "the largest continuous audience ever possessed by a man who was neither politician nor divine."

Anyway, it had been in Winchell's column that I first read the phrase, "Whee The People."

I ended my letter to Caen, "So, if you will be so kind as to give Winchell back the phrase *he* created, I'll give you back what *you* claim is yours."

A week later, Caen wrote back with a big "Oops," apologizing for accusing me of theft and adding, "Well pal, you nailed me. You are correct. I admit I swiped 'Whee The People' from Winchell." (Today, with both Winchell and Caen gone and me happily retired, the *Honolulu Advertiser*'s "Show Biz" columnist Wayne Harada uses the phrase—with my blessings.)

Eventually, I got to meet Caen, and we both laughed about the incident. Moreover, we both admitted that we stole stuff from Winchell, as did so many of the columnists in America who wrote in the three-dot format.

Fade out, fade in: years later, sometime in the early 1960s, a large throng of Honolulu media gathered at Hickam Field in Honolulu, waiting for President Dwight Eisenhower to arrive. He was on his way to Japan when riots broke out in that country. As a result, he was advised to turn around and cancel his Japan agenda.

Honolulu was quickly chosen for a bit of R&R for Ike. Most reporters at the *Advertiser* were on the "welcoming committee" at Hickam on this bright, sunny day. My assignment was to gather color items.

After the first plane landed, a small knot of people was gathered near the steps leading down from the aircraft. One of the men seemed to be the center of attention and was doing most of the talking. He wore a snap-brim hat and blue suit.

"Who's that character?" I asked the reporter next to me.

"You mean you don't know Walter Winchell?" he replied; "he's only the most famous columnist in America."

At the time, Winchell was in the twilight of his fantastic career. In my eyes, however, he was still the giant of giants—the most popular and powerful columnist journalism ever spawned. Not only was Winchell the inventor of the three-dot column, he was also the creator of a language that was absolutely original. He was one of a kind.

After Eisenhower's arrival, the media got on buses and headed for a press conference at Camp Smith, the Pacific's military headquarters. On my bus, Winchell and I stood side by side.

Finally, I had my opportunity to talk to the great Walter Winchell.

He knew instantly that I was a fan and admirer. He told me interesting tales about being with Ike on this trip. He said he'd be happy to see me anytime during his week's stay in Hawaii.

The next night, we met for dinner at Don the Beachcomber at

the International Market Place in Waikiki. That turned out to be our evening routine for the entire week. Being with him was like viewing a daily one-man Winchell show. I kept asking questions, and he was a nonstop talker. We made a perfect match.

I wish I'd had a recorder going during our conversations. Winchell shared tremendous tales about celebrities, the underworld and, of course, himself. He admitted he was sometimes an SOB. Told me about the many times he was double-crossed, about the stars he made famous, and how he kept otherwise doomed Broadway shows open with his constant plugging.

He was so powerful that just one mention in his column about a young comedy team, Rowan & Martin, took them out of the rundown Miami nightclub they were playing for just a few hundred dollars a week to a $10,000 New York engagement overnight. That launched the duo's long career in television.

The last night Winchell was in Honolulu, I was a little late coming to the restaurant. When I arrived, he was fuming.

"Where the hell ya been?" he snarled.

"Sorry, Walter," I apologized. "I was at the *Advertiser* writing a column about Honolulu that I thought you might like to use."

I handed him the column. He put on his glasses, drew the table lamp over and began to read. When he finished, he had a tear in his eye.

"You did this for me?" he asked. "It's a terrific column. I really appreciate this. And I will definitely run it. Also, I love the title, 'Things I Never Knew About Hawaii Till Now.'"

I smiled at Walter and said, "I have to admit, I really didn't write this. I just updated it. It was written long ago—1938, to be exact."

Winchell looked puzzled. "Then who's the author?" he asked.

I smiled and looked straight into his eyes.

"You!"

Sadly, at the time of his death on February 20, 1972, Winchell was practically a forgotten man. His daughter, Walda, was the only mourner at his funeral, and only 150 people attended a special memorial service held on what would have been his seventy-fifth birthday.

The obituaries portrayed him as a relic who was way past his prime. His friends tried to rename the traffic island in New York's Times Square after him, but that admirable attempt was met with bureaucratic indifference.

"Nothing he left behind seemed to endure," wrote biographer Neal Gabler. "His name faded—the name he had worked so hard to burn into the public consciousness."

No matter. I know that I will never forget Walter Winchell. He was one of a kind, an icon of our nation. As Gabler wrote, "[Winchell] was the promise of American freedom and uninhibited bounce; he was Americanism symbolized in a nose-thumbing at the portentousness of the great; he released them for fifteen minutes once a week from the fear of oppression; he was the defender of the American faith."

Meeting Winchell and spending a week with him was, without a doubt, one of the biggest thrills of my journalistic career.

Fast Fact: Walter Winchell

Walter Winchell spent five seasons narrating the ABC TV series *The Untouchables*. He was reportedly paid $25,000 an episode for his services.

THIRTY-SEVEN

Short Takes

Jim Nabors

Jim Nabors has made Hawaii his home for more than thirty years. It's been a quiet Island life for "Mr. Gollleeee," though he does emerge publicly once in a while to entertain locally or attend various social functions. However, for many years, Nabors has kept a busy entertainment schedule on the Mainland.

But ever since his life-threatening kidney transplant a few years ago, he's cut way back on his traveling.

"I'm lucky to be alive," he told me. "So, I'm enjoying everything one day at a time."

Jim has a number of business interests that keep him busy, including his large ranch in Hana, Maui, where he grows macadamia nuts. He also owns the *Gomer Pyle* TV show that made him a star and still plays in reruns all over the world.

"What I like especially about Hawaii are the people," he said. "They leave me alone. They are kind, sweet and nice, and they treat me like I belong here. It's the aloha spirit."

And Jim gives back. Big time. For years, he has starred in the annual "Merry Christmas with Friends and Nabors" charity show at the Hawaii Theatre, never once charging for his services.

With Jim, what you see is what you get. No airs, no phony baloney stuff. He's just plain down to earth and friendly. But privately, he's definitely not that goofy character he played on *Gomer*. He's a college grad with a degree in business who's blessed with that great voice.

Johnny Carson

During one of my visits to Vegas, my friend Herb McDonald, chief of public relations at the Sahara, set me up with an interview with the legendary TV star Johnny Carson. I was asked to wait in his dressing room. It was a memorable interview, all right. I'll never forget it! When Carson walked in after his show and saw me sitting there, he asked, "What can I do for you?" When I told him I was there for an interview, he acted like he didn't know and suddenly remembered with, "Oh, yes."

He paused and then asked, "So what would you like to know?"

I forget exactly what I asked him at that moment, but I'll never forget his reply. He said, "That's the dumbest fucking question I ever heard."

With that I stood up, put my notebook in my pocket and said, "Thank you, Mr. Carson," and headed for the door.

He stopped me, apologized, and asked me to come back and sit down. From then on he was polite and communicative, but cool. I sensed something was bugging him, and so I stayed only a few minutes before once again bidding him aloha.

Yousuf Karsh

During my early years of fatherhood, I was an avid shutterbug. So when I heard that the legendary Canadian photographer Yousuf Karsh was staying at the Kahala Hilton, I quickly called for an interview. He was a small, bald, charming man with courtly manners. Karsh was born in Turkey in 1908, and he and his family emigrated when he was fifteen, thanks to a sponsorship from an uncle, who was a photographer living in Canada.

Although Karsh lensed the great personalities of his time—King George VI, Norway's King Hakkon, military leaders, George Bernard Shaw, Noel Coward, H.G. Wells and many others—it was his photograph of Winston Churchill that brought him worldwide fame.

He told me how it happened.

"In 1941 Churchill was visiting Ottawa," he said. "Canada's Prime Minister, Mackenzie King, arranged for me to photograph Churchill in the speaker's chamber following his speech in the House of Commons.

"When Churchill arrived, he growled, 'Why wasn't I told of this?' But he consented to a brief session. I only had a few short minutes to get my picture. I used a special rubber bulb that I kept in my hand, usually behind my back. When I squeezed, the camera snapped.

"Suddenly, Churchill stuck a big cigar in his mouth and lit it. He really didn't want to be photographed. I walked up to him and, without warning, yanked the cigar out of his mouth. Churchill looked like he was going to eat me alive. I quickly squeezed the bulb. The shot was taken. That picture rewarded me with international fame, and was used over and over as a symbol of England's fighting spirit and determination to crush the Nazis."

During our interview, I took a photo of Karsh. When I showed it to him later, I asked him to comment on my photography. He studied it for a moment, smiled slyly and then deadpanned, "You are, without a doubt, the world's second-best photographer."

France Nuyen

France was eighteen when she won the coveted role of Liat in the 1958 film *South Pacific,* which starred Rossano Brazzi and Mitzi Gaynor and was made entirely in Hawaii. The classic Rodgers and Hammerstein musical was directed by Joshua Logan, who also directed the Broadway production. The film was based on James Michener's novel.

I was on the movie set a number of times, gathering tidbits for my column. I'll never forget watching the scene when Rossano sang "Some Enchanted Evening" to Gaynor. The music and singing, of course, were pre-recorded, and the director called for a number of takes before he was satisfied. Such an important production was a very big deal for Hawaii in those days.

France was a curious bundle of joy. She seemed interested in everything about Hawaii. For a while, whenever time permitted, I was her tour guide and studio chaperone. I was like a father figure to her, and we became good friends. Even today, we still correspond. Over the years, I was an occasional sounding board when she wanted to talk about her romances or marriages.

During one of her visits to Honolulu, after her success in the lead role in 1958's *The World of Suzie Wong* on Broadway, she lived with my family for a few months. She was quite the character. One afternoon, as we drove along Kapiolani Boulevard, passing cars started honking. It was a sound seldom heard in Hawaii. Suddenly, I looked to my right. France had her body half out the window, totally topless, smiling and waving to everyone. It's a wonder some of the cars didn't bang into each other! She was definitely a free spirit in those days.

Leonard Bernstein

One weekend, the great musical genius Leonard Bernstein stopped in Honolulu for a concert at the Waikiki Shell. He and the entire New York Philharmonic were on their way to engagements in Asia. The pre-show press conference took place on the lawn of the Royal Hawaiian. Media people filled 50 or 60 chairs, with more standing to the side. Bernstein sat in front of this group fielding questions. Suddenly I had an idea. I grabbed a chair, dragged it across the lawn, placed it right next to the famed maestro and sat down facing the crowd.

Bernstein, naturally puzzled by this intrusion, turned to me and asked, "Can I help you?"

"Not really," I said quietly. "But I have something important to tell you."

"What is it?" he whispered back.

Looking furtively around as if protecting some great secret, I said, "My mother makes the greatest pickled herring you ever tasted."

Bernstein was game. Playing the straight man, he said, "When can I have some?"

"It depends," I replied.

"Depends on what?" he asked.

"On your concert tonight. Do a good job and I'll see that you get some pickled herring right after the show." With that I shook his hand, got up, dragged the chair back across the lawn and left.

That evening, the Shell was packed. It was the first and only time

I witnessed the great maestro in action. What a showman. He was mesmerizing. His performance and the Philharmonic's music were flawless. Backstage after the concert, it felt like a political headquarters on election night. As I wended my way to Bernstein's dressing room with a bucket full of herring, I encountered the Shell's manager, Marshall Turkin.

"What's in that thermos?" he wanted to know

"Herring." I kept walking.

"For what?" Marshall asked.

"I'm giving it to Bernstein."

"Are you planning to embarrass the maestro?"

"No, silly, he's expecting this."

"I'm going along to make sure," he said.

The corridor leading to the star's dressing room was crowded with people wanting a few minutes with Leonard Bernstein. As Marshall and I waited outside, the door opened a crack and his personal dresser peeked out. Wordlessly, I held up the aluminum bucket. She frantically motioned me towards the dressing room, asking the others to let me by.

Inside, Bernstein was sitting at his make-up table. "Is that it?" he asked.

"Yes," I said, smiling, "and you certainly deserve it. You were just great tonight."

As I dished some of the herring into a small bowl, he eyed it ravishingly.

Then he cut a piece of herring in half and closed his eyes, chewing slowly. There was total silence in the dressing room.

"Well?" I asked.

He grinned and said, "'Daphne and Chloe.'"

"What's that?" I asked.

"Schmuck!" he laughed. "That was the next-to-last piece I played tonight. Delicious and sensuous, just like this herring. It's perfect!"

Leonard Bernstein quickly devoured all of the herring along with the pumpernickel bread I had brought along. "Tell your mother she makes the best pickled herring in the Pacific," he said.

EPILOGUE

My Hawaii

Well, here we are—the final chapter. I have mixed feelings about it. The process of writing this book has been quite a journey for me—a wonderful trip down memory lane, renewing old acquaintances—friendships, really—and reliving so many special experiences.

Although I wanted to write a book for a long time, I was always a bit apprehensive about it. Frankly, I didn't think I could do it. Over the years, I talked to potential ghostwriters, but for one reason or another, it never came to fruition.

My wife, Patty, however, kept nudging me along.

"These are *your* stories," she reminded me over and over again. "I know you can do it."

Finally I sat myself down at the computer and sweated out a few sample chapters, which I then submitted to George Engebretson, the publisher at Watermark Publishing. George, who'd grown up reading my columns in the *Advertiser,* said, "Let's do it." Just like that. This gave me a shot of confidence. And he added, "We'll do it right, too." He assigned a talented (and patient) editor, Lance Tominaga, to put up with me and asked Frederika Bain to handle some of the research. I can't thank them enough for their help in making this book happen.

Every book has an ending. I thought long and hard about how I wanted to end mine. How do I best summarize all my experiences and relationships with the rich and famous—these celebrities that I have been fortunate to meet and know?

Then it hit me.

The common thread throughout these pages—and in the greatest moments in my life—is not really the celebrities themselves. Instead, the true star of this book is what first enthralled me so many years ago after as I stepped off the *Lurline*. It's what captured the hearts of people like Marlon Brando, Frank Sinatra, Elvis Presley and Red Skelton. It's what I had in common with Sammy Davis, Jr., Albert Finney, Henry Kaiser and Max Winter.

Hawaii.

I would like to share with you one of my favorite columns from my days with the *Honolulu Advertiser*. It originally appeared in the late 1960s. I think it suitably expresses my love for this wild, exotic and impossibly beautiful paradise called Hawaii—my Island home.

Those who may think they have very little to be thankful for, look around you and enjoy the beauty of Hawaii ... See the palms of Waikiki, stately sentinels protecting a boulevard of frivolity ... Strange mixtures of the International Market Place ... The happy hodge-podge of races represented, rainbow-like among Waikiki's beach boys ... Sunset Beach, that watery turmoil which churns and boils like a washing machine for the spirit ... How much we who live here take for granted—but reawaken when showing a visiting friend around who appreciates and marvels at the gem-green of the land ... The fourteen-karat gold of the people ... The classic curve of the many beaches on all the islands ... Or the fragrance of the lei stands and the historic richness of Iolani Palace ... Nature's busy fingers weaving Kapiolani's tapestry. An astonishing creation full of subtle mysteries ... The passion of the soft tropical winds sighing through the trees ... Birds scaling the blue heights, soaring and dipping their ballet-like maneuvers over Kapiolani Park ... The sounds of music drifting from Blaisdell's concert hall ... Trans-oceanic glittering palaces, quietly gliding in and out of our harbor ... The serpent of traffic snaking along congested freeways ... The sickening crunch of metal signifying a traffic mishap ... The fading solar fire of twilight's blue haze ... The magnificent panorama of Waikiki from the heights of the Sheraton's Hanohano Room ... Have you ever seen Honolulu from far offshore while sailing above the ink-blue clouds of ocean? ... Or heard Honolulu while you are out there beyond the reef? The white-winged racing boats bouncing on the sea like exploding popcorn ... Among the many faces of Honolulu, one that's particularly special is Chinatown ... The streets narrow and deep like the creases in the work-worn faces of the aging ... A spirit as brassy and buoyant as 10,000 firecrackers swinging on the tail of a paper demon ... The atmosphere as strong as the smell of the fresh fish lying on beds of ice in the open markets ... The mystery of it all—exotic as the uses of the herbs which dangle like dragon tails from the storefronts of Chinatown ... Hotel Street's bizarre character ... Hawaii is acknowledged as the islands of romance. But, one island—Niihau—is the last repository of unsullied Hawaiiana ... Its people still ride on horseback in the era of the orbit, stubbornly living from the ripe red soil in the age of the TV dinner ... Niihau—where only Hawaiian is spoken—out of context ... Out of tune ... And truly, out of this oh-so-modern world ... And to those who don't think Menehunes exist, well, I think they're wrong ... Who can listen to or look at a mynah bird without feeling that here indeed is a rascal—a winged one, I grant you—but nonetheless a Menehune ... Those chatter-box pranksters, the bane of late-sleeping tourists ... The nemeses of army worms, the delight of shoppers who are startled, and then amused when a shrill whistle and a raucous "Hi beautiful!" comes screeching from a bamboo cage or high up in the trees ... Kapiolani Boulevard before daybreak, as a city truck deposits those rubber cones—spaced evenly, to build new lanes of traffic ... Weekends in Hawaii ... When people go to the beaches to warm their bodies ... A family huddles around a hibachi, probing with chopsticks that miraculously never seem to catch fire ... A father romping at the water's edge, carefully edging his timid child closer to the toothpaste foam of the playful Pacific ... Young girls, self-contained in their brief bathing suits ... Elderly tourists, creaking with age and a life of toil enjoying their savings with a trip to Paradise and thinking, "Why did I wait so long?" ... Kalaupapa, once the famed peninsula of the damned ... Kalaupapa—the cross of Damien the Martyr... Once a garbage heap for the body, an incinerator for the soul ... Now a fading retreat from the non-understanding world ... The East-West Center is another part of my Hawaii—out where Manoa Valley spills in leafy green down to Moiliili ... Crisp angled buildings—sharp and well defined ... The East-West Center, symbol of man's hopes for peace in the Pacific— a peace which, hopefully, will move tidal wave-like into other ethnic oceans of the world. The Center, a point of light, trying hopefully to burst through the smothering night of bureaucracy ... Just a quick glimpse of my Hawaii.

Writing this book has been a wonderful experience—a leisurely, nostalgic drive down memory lane. One of the first things I found out about journalism is that it does not offer many monetary rewards. You just don't get rich in this racket.

But if you're lucky, you receive something else.

For me, it offered a seat on the fifty-yard line of life. It afforded me a fantastic opportunity to meet and know some of the world's most famous people.

And the greatest of them all was Mister and Missus Hawaii.

Aloha!

About the Author

Eddie Sherman has been Hawaii's best-read three-dot columnist since he began his newspaper career in 1955. The Boston native arrived in the Islands in wartime as a 17-year-old sheet metal worker at Pearl Harbor. After working in Island radio and nightspots and performing for five years in New England comedy clubs, he spent more than four decades as a newspaper columnist for *The Honolulu Advertiser* and *MidWeek*. He currently lives in Honolulu with his wife, Patty.

INDEX

Ali, Muhammad, 75, 81, *169*, 188-191
Amalu, Sonny, 207-210
Ariyoshi, George, 105, 135-136, 140

Beatty, Clyde, *74*, 181-182
Belafonte, Harry, 154
Berle, Milton, *164*, 200-201
Bernstein, Leonard, *168*, 235-236
Blaisdell, Neal, 129
Boone, Richard, 12, *155*, 204-206
Brando, Marlon, 5, 19, 81, 136, 146-154, 160, *161*, 162, 171-176, 204, 207, 238
Bruce, Lenny, 142-145
Buchwach, Buck, 30, 31-32, 82-83, 84, 89-90, 193, 194-195
Burns, John, 12, 98, 129, 134-135

Caen, Herb, 227, 228-229
Cantor, Eddie, 1-2, 212
Carson, Johnny, 47, 107, 233
Cass, Peggy, 109
Chaplin, George, 76-77, 78, 175, 209, 225
Clavell, James, 114-117
Crosby, Norm, 26-28, 63
Cunningham, Owen, 20, 21-22

Davis, Sammy, Jr., 5, 84, *164*, 211-214, 217, 239
Dempsey, Jack, *74*, 181-183
Dornberger, Walter, 224-226
Douglas, Kirk, 131, 132, 192
Dundee, Angelo, 188-191

Ellis, Marjorie, 10-13, *62*
Esposito, Matt, 76

Finnegan, Bill, 105
Finney, Albert, 5, 39-42, 239
Ford, John, 17, 118-123, 197
Freeman, Leonard, 97-98, 99-102, 104, 130, *158*, 204, 206

Gabler, Neal, 227-228, 231
Garland, Judy, 5, 84, 124-127, 196
Godfrey, Arthur, 34-38, *69*
Graziano, Rocky, 150

Harada, Wayne, 228
Harrington, Stan, 217, 218-219
Harris, Hunter, *62*
Harris, Richard, 121

Hepburn, Katherine, 88
Hickey, Mike, 221-222
Ho, Don, 53-55, *71*, 129, 133, 139
Hope, Bob, 50-52, 200

J. Akuhead Pupule, 22-23, 30, 68, 94, 142
Jacobs, Ron, 94, 95

Kahanamoku, Duke, 35, 68, 177
Kaiser, Henry J., *91-96*, 239
Karsh, Yousuf, 233-234
Kashfi, Anna, 171-172
Kelly, Gene, 57, 58, 111-112, 113
King, Paul, 99-100
Koch, Howard, 85-87
Krauss, Bob, 73, 107-109

Lancaster, Burt, 84, 131, 132
Lee, Kui, 77, 128-133
LeRoy, Mervyn, 87-88, 89, 122, 163
Lord, Jack, 78, 97-106, *158*, 202, 206
Loren, Sophia, 215-216

MacLaine, Shirley, 132
Manilow, Barry, 46-47
Marciano, Rocky, 5, 56-58, 75, 167
Martin, Dean, *64*, 84, 86, 154
McDonald, Herb, 233
Mehau, Larry, 134-141, 157
Meredith, Burgess, *91-92*, 136, *166*, 192-195
Midler, Bette, 43-49
Miller, Flash, 53, 148
Minelli, Liza, 214
Moffatt, Tom, 94, 221, 222-223
Montalban, Ricardo, 159
Mossman, Sterling, 53, 128

Nabors, Jim, 232
Newton, Wayne, 80-81
Nuyen, France, 152, *156*, 234-235

Oberon, Merle, 4-5
O'Connor, Donald, 56-58, 75, 103, 196, 197

Paar, Jack, 107-110, 158
Paladino, Rocky, 25, 26, 29
Parker, Col. Tom, *72*, 76-81, 220
Preminger, Otto, 192-195
Presley, Elvis, 5, 19, *72*, *73*, 76-81, 131, 207, 220, 238

Quinn, Anthony, *168*

Rackin, Marty, 121-122, 177-178
Resnick, Joe, 185-187
Robinson, Sugar Ray, *167*, 217-219
Robotnick, Bessie, 6-7, *64*, *65*, 91, 152-154
Ruff, Bob, 148-149
Ryan, Peggy, 43, 56-57, 103, 121, 152-153, 196-198, 216

Sands, Tommy, 220-223
Sevey, Bob, *159*
Sheehan, Ed, 30-31, 41-42
Sherman, Patty, 1-2, 109, *168*, 237
Sherman, Shawn, 138-139
Sinatra, Frank, 5, 19, 70, 81, 82-90, 207, 214, 222, 238
Skelton, Red, 143, 165, 178, 199-203, 239
Smith, Liz, 175-176
Soo, Jack, *68*, 111-113 (see also Suzuki, Goro)
Suzuki, Goro, 23-25 (see also Soo, Jack)

Taka, Miiko, *166*
Takahashi, Sakae, 98-99
Taylor, Elizabeth, 185
Todd, Mike, 185-187
Topol, 102-103
Tracy, Spencer, 88

Umeki, Miyoshi, 232-233
Uycatel, Hy, 87

von Trapp, Hedwig, *68*

Wallis, Hal, 128-133
Wayne, John, 118, 122, 123, 125, *166*, 192, 193
Weisman, Len, 104
Williams, Dick, 124-125
Wilson, Earl, *164*
Winchell, Walter, 107, *170*, 177, 227-231
Winter, Max, *74*, 179-184, 239

Yamamoto, Hiro, 98-99, 100

Zulu, 103-105